Fatal Attraction

Reflections on the Alliance with the United States

Bruce Grant

Black Inc.

Published by Black Inc.
An imprint of Schwartz Publishing

Level 5, 289 Flinders Lane
Melbourne Victoria 3000 Australia
email: enquiries@blackincbooks.com
http://www.blackincbooks.com

National Library of Australia Cataloguing-in-Publication entry:

Grant, Bruce, 1925- .
Fatal attraction : Reflections on the Alliance with the United States

ISBN 0 9750769 3 0.

1. National security - Australia. 2. Alliances. 3. Australia - Foreign relations - United States. 4. United States - Foreign relations - Australia. I. Title.

327.94073

Book design: Thomas Deverall

Printed in Australia by Griffin Press

Contents

Introduction

This short book, which is in the nature of an extended essay, is an inquiry into Australian foreign policy, prompted by contemporary events. The counter-attack on terrorism that followed the terrorist attacks on New York and Washington on September 11, 2001 has exposed a weakness in our alliance with the United States, which is our most important security partnership. Australia was drawn into a military commitment initiated by the Bush administration in Washington that was neither in our interests nor perhaps, a growing number of Americans are discovering, in the interests of the United States. The invasion and occupation of Iraq, in particular, has divided both countries to a degree not seen since the controversial war in Vietnam thirty years ago. In Australia, the way the Howard government has defended the commitment has touched a nerve of national sentiment, not just at the level of public opinion but among those responsible for the conduct of defence and foreign policy.

At the time of writing, governments in Washington

and Canberra (and London) and their diplomatic and military agencies, including those responsible for intelligence, are at odds with each other over who got it right and who got it wrong. It is not a pretty sight, but it is instructive. Success has many authors, failure none. It is disingenuous to attribute the fall-out to democracy at work. Servants of the state, whether they are overt or covert, do not break with long-held customs of silence and discretion unless the circumstances are unusual, either personally or nationally. The unusual public circumstances in this case are twofold. One is that the Iraq mission was badly managed and has turned out to be counter-productive, giving the al Qaeda organisation responsible for the September 11 attacks a recruiting boost. The other is that for the first time in our history (in Britain's, too, I understand, and possibly the United States') secret intelligence has been publicly exposed by governments to justify their decision to go to war.

The political consequences are hard to predict. It might be useful for hard-pressed governments if the intelligence on which they claim to have based their decisions is now shown to be faulty. On the other hand, the public is not impressed with a display of distemper in high places, and there is really only one answer to the question of responsibility for sending men and women abroad to fight. Governments are responsible. The act of going to war cannot be delegated. The intelligence agencies, like other arms of government, provide information and assessment, but it is the responsibility of governments to weigh these against other sources and make policy accordingly. What happened in the case of Iraq is that governments used the credibility of secret intelligence to back publicly their decision to go to war. It turned out the intelligence they exposed was in part faulty, but whether this was because it was bad intelligence or intelligence skewed to fit the needs of committed governments remains an open question.

Over time, the way a country uses force to protect and promote its interests begins to shape its identity. So an inquiry into Australian foreign policy needs to establish how we got where we are; we need to know what we are capable of, when this crisis is over. Australia's peculiarity is that we have developed an ardent military tradition based on expeditions abroad, while being incapable of undertaking a primary responsibility of nationhood, which is to look after yourself. Foreign policy was hampered by being required to ensure that it did not upset those great and powerful friends, first Britain and then the United States, who were expected to come to our assistance when we were in need.

Our experience in Vietnam caused some heartburn and rethinking, which showed eventually in a significant shift in our defence priorities. A burst of regional foreign policy initiatives during the Hawke-Keating period – the Cambodian peace settlement, the creation of Asia-Pacific Economic Cooperation (APEC) and the ASEAN Regional Forum (ARF) – were in part a response to the

1987 defence White Paper, which said in layman's language that, except in the event of war involving nuclear-armed adversaries, Australia was capable of defending itself. This liberated Australian foreign policy to take initiatives which, at first, the United States did not regard with favour but which became established as a framework for security in our region.

Australia was emboldened to take these initiatives because the United States was in an unusually strong, secure position. It was, as our foreign minister at the time, Gareth Evans, once remarked, "a dream run" for foreign policy. The United States had emerged from the Cold War as the sole surviving military superpower. It was also politically and even culturally dominant, taking into account the global impact of the English language and popular American culture. Within a short time, once the constraints and demands of the Cold War were released, its economy recovered. Significantly, a new balance of power that would seek to counter its dominance did not emerge. Americans, haunted by the sense that they were vulnerable to attack by those who feared and envied them, could put to rest their longing for invulnerability and begin to co-operate with the rest of the world. For a time, this seemed possible. The eight years of Clinton were not conclusive but they did suggest to non-Americans that a more relaxed, accommodating and inclusive United States was emerging.

I wrote at that time in a book about the United States that it had the opportunity to become the first truly global power in human history, if it understood the forces at work in the post-Cold War period. It seemed to me, as it did to many, that the end of the Cold War offered the world an opportunity to dismantle the huge military machine that had been assembled over decades of readiness for war and that the United States, as a liberal democracy, could lead in the twenty-first century by revisiting the issues of global governance and human rights, health, education and prosperity of the world's people that had been left on the table after the Second World War.

The Bush administration signalled with its proposal for national missile defence and rejection of several important international conventions, long before the terrorist attacks, that it intended to assert American power more aggressively. Its conduct of the war on terrorism confirmed that approach and amplified it, raising difficult questions for its allies. So to enter the contemporary debate requires more than a discussion of the current "war" on terrorism. As the Vietnam War created an opportunity for fresh thinking, it is appropriate now to raise the broader issue of how Australia should manage its military alliance with the United States and, further, what role should the armed forces of states, especially powerful states, have in determining the nature of the world we live in.

In this sombre world in terrorism's shadow, Australia's military alliance with the United States has received a new lease of life. It is at the heart of the commitments we have made, not contemplated before, in Afghanistan and Iraq. It overwhelms our political discourse, creating a divisive debate not experienced since the war in Vietnam. It diverts our resources to security requirements that, if experience is any guide, will not be quickly satisfied. It raises questions about our place in our region, whether that is the South Pacific, south-east Asia, East Asia or the Asia-Pacific. It touches again a sensitive spot in the Australian psyche, whether, embattled as an outpost of Western values at the bottom of the world, we are doomed forever to be grateful to a powerful state engaged vigorously in the world at every level and pleased to have us at its side. I once playfully described this role as spear carrier to the chief, thinking that it would not last. And it asks, finally, a question that has long nagged at the conscience of countries that consider themselves to be civilised: whether force used in the national interest over time has more influence in shaping national identity than the visions and dreams of peace-loving citizens.

Australians are easily impressed by the power of the United States. Our journalists and our politicians on visits to Washington are convinced they are in the centre of the world. We have adopted unthinkingly many of the values of its commercial, democratic society. Being one step behind the United States is sufficient to ensure a level of accomplishment here. Yet, in foreign policy, our approaches are fundamentally different. The United States does not regard itself as another nation-state in a global system. It regards itself as a model to be followed. Australia, by contrast, is guided by the need to work co-operatively with others. It will never have the kind of power that the United States now has, because we live in a region that we cannot expect to subdue in the way the United States has gained supremacy in its hemisphere.

Australia is an effective, middle-sized country, with some experience now in working out ways of living at peace with our neighbours. We are politically stable and our economy ranks usually just outside the top ten in the world. We have shown that we have the capacity to organise and co-operate with others on important global issues; examples include the Australia Group, established to monitor precursors of chemical weapons; the Cairns Group, for fair trade in agriculture; and our role as chair of a like-minded group of 65 countries that helped to get the numbers for the International Criminal Court. We have shown, too, that we can take regional initiatives, as in the formation of APEC, ARF and the United Nations peace plan for Cambodia. We have a need to be co-operative on foreign policy issues with the United States, but no need to be subservient. On the contrary, our promise is that globally minded middle powers like us can be the midwives of peace and prosperity in the twenty-first century. We have every reason to encourage the United States to be more like us, co-operative, flexible and interested in finding a constructive solution to the turbulence of the contemporary world.

This book is written to enhance Australia's alliance with the United States, not to undermine it. It recognises, however, that the military connection has a fatal attraction for each of us. It is tempting when you are powerful to go to war to get your way and it is encouraging to have supportive allies. It is reassuring for Australia to have the complexities of international politics and the ambiguities of our region simplified by the exertion of American power. The hard task ahead is to use the alliance, not to ignore or subvert the emerging international and regional regimes, but to build them.

TURBULENCE

In the short term, the uncertainties of the exciting and puzzling world that emerged from the Cold War seemed to be resolved by the terrorist attacks on New York and Washington on September 11, 2001. It was often said at the time, and not usually contested, that the world would never be the same again. The collapse of the twin towers of the World Trade Center was the most spectacular event in the lifetime of its global audience and is already established as an iconic image of the twenty-first century. As a production or demonstration effect, which is often said to be the purpose of terrorism, it was brilliant. But its lasting effect on how power is disposed and managed in the world is still emerging. It has certainly had an effect on the United States, especially on its military forces and its economy, and it has had a lesser but substantial effect on all governments, especially in the West. It has also had a moral effect.

It has jolted sentiment from the pursuit of pleasure and making money to contemplate other values. Some see an era of terror and counter-terror as the beginning of another Cold War marking the end of globalisation, not only because of the actual economic effect, especially on the insurance, aviation and tourist industries, but because of the psychological effect. Life is serious and earnest again, as it was then, when the world was caught up in an ideological conflict about the right way to live. The trivial urge to consume, which is the genius of capitalism, and the drive to reach out, interact and network, which is the genius of globalisation, have been checked by the state asserting its power, especially its military power, but also as intervention for security reasons in everyday life.

Was the movement to "one world" merely post-Cold War euphoria, a kind of fantasy brought on by the outbreak of peace? The world had been at war for half a century – from 1939, the beginning of the Second World War, to 1989, the end of the Cold War, with a break of only about eighteen months between. The executive is strengthened in war and the legislature is weakened. Presidents and prime ministers are given latitude because of secrecy and contingency, domestic issues are subjected to the test of the national interest and, in any case, the public is itself committed to wartime objectives, even if its commitment may flag over a long period. The end being clear, the means are not closely examined.

When peace breaks out, a reversal occurs. People's dreams surface and the private sector, held in check during war by the state's security needs, is released.

Powerful individuals with private agendas, pressure groups and non-government organisations with an intense dedication to narrow interests, and revived opposition parties do their best to defeat or confound government policies they do not like. Governments have to redefine the national interest on each specific issue and persuade a sceptical public that the means proposed are appropriate. Libertarians come into their own. The grand moral narratives that the state had constructed, justifying itself, blaming others, are torn to shreds.

In addition, as the end of the twentieth century approached, there was a surge of *fin de siècle* nostalgia and futuristic thinking. The old imponderables surfaced, including questions of human origin and destiny. A millennium put an even greater strain on the public's imagination, especially as the twentieth century had been so violent, casting doubt on those theories of progress that came to us from the nineteenth. Sydney, for example, celebrated the turn of the millennium with the word "Eternity", which had a highly eccentric, local connotation. For half a century the word had been appearing on pavements in chalk, mystifying Sydneysiders until 1985, when the author was discovered: Arthur Stace, a criminal and reformed alcoholic. His message, whatever its meaning, was now emblazoned to the world.

Even when globalisation was at its hectic high point in the 1990s, and the nation-state was thought by some to be doomed, there was a view that it was, for all its sensational effects, nothing new, merely a revival of past efforts to move beyond the geographical confinement of territory and the idea of political sovereignty. The nineteenth century saw a similar spread of free trade, investment, migration, and a revolution in global information due to the electric telegraph. This differed only in speed and quantity from today's global market in goods and services and an information explosion on the internet. Moreover, it also created uncertainty and ended abruptly, as nation-states competed for renewed supremacy in the new conditions, leading to the First World War. The world had seemed then to be on the brink of discovering how to pursue prosperity and remain peaceful, but powerful nations had broken ranks and created chaos. The mutual self-interest of economic interdependence had then, as now, led us to believe that wars would no longer be fought, because they were unprofitable, which had led to disillusionment. The dislocation of economic and political life had led us then, as now, to believe that the nation-state stood in the way of peace and progress.

The *Economist* concluded in 1930, after the crash of Wall Street but before the German people turned to Adolf Hitler:

> The supreme difficulty of our generation … is that our achievements on the economic plane of life have outstripped our progress on the political plane

> to such an extent that our economics and our politics are perpetually falling out of gear with one another. On the economic plane, the world has been organised into a single, all-embracing unit of activity. On the political plane, it has not only remained partitioned into sixty or seventy sovereign national States, but the national units have been growing smaller and more numerous and the national consciousness more acute. The tension between these two antithetical tendencies has been producing a series of jolts and jars and smashes in the social life of humanity …

It is even truer today that global thinking and organisation are necessary, not just to manage an increasingly global economy, but to cope with political tendencies that threaten to jolt and jar the social life of humanity once again. The spread of weapons of mass destruction is one such tendency. Another is a range of environmental pressures that are oblivious to national boundaries. Another is demographic imbalance, with high birth rates in poor countries and declining rates in wealthy countries. Another is a combination of drug smuggling, terrorism and international crime. So, even without taking into account the need for co-operation between states to keep the machinery of the world's mundane transactions turning, the need for states to co-operate globally in their own interests would seem to be self-evident. Yet the assertion of military power by the

United States and Australia has raised doubts about this globalising process, creating a rift among those major states who have the fate of the world in their hands.

My own view is that September 11, 2001 does not mark the end of the globalising process and that security issues that confront the world today can only be understood and dealt with in a global framework. In a real, not just a celebratory, sense, the twenty-first century is a new era in world politics. The reasons are essentially two: a truly global dimension of relations between states and a change in the nature of the state itself. It is a simple theme at one level and complex at another. The simple theme is that the world is becoming a single unit. The means of achieving both war and peace are global. The way of doing business is becoming global, as is the pursuit of knowledge. But human beings are not organised to act globally. That is the complex theme.

*

Global tendencies capture the imagination, but the nation-state remains for most people the means through which human beings act publicly, including internationally. Whether they like it or not, most people live as part of a nation and are bound by the laws made by the state on their behalf. Many regard this as normal and indeed the mainspring of emotions they hold dear, like patriotism, duty and honour, but in a global context these emotions are losing their power and efficacy.

The nation-state, as we have known it for more than three centuries, is restricted in the way it approaches the people and the governments of other states. It tends to be exclusive and suspicious, often aggressive. It is jealous of its control of people and territory and its authority to represent those people to others in the world outside its territory. It has begun to accept international obligations to protect and promote its interests and the human rights of its citizens, yet states are themselves often, through their instruments of law enforcement, the police and military forces, gross abusers of human rights. In addition, the rational use of force, which has long been a defining characteristic of the state, arising from its duty to protect its territory and its citizens and to promote its interests, is no longer self-evidently effective, either as a right or a means. Weapons, especially, but not solely, nuclear weapons, have become so destructive that their victims are increasingly civilians, not members of the armed services recruited to defend the state. So while the modern state has shown itself to be an effective way of socialising people and an efficient way of creating wealth, there are indications in the contemporary world that it is under stress. The result is that, almost daily, the world we live in has outbreaks of contradictory symptoms.

Against the global tendencies are acute withdrawal symptoms, a turning inward to sub-national forms of identity and to religion and culture. Relief at the end of the Cold War from the threat of a third world war in the twentieth century has not been accompanied by a more relaxing peace in the twenty-first. Whether or not there has been a statistical increase in conflict, it has seemed so, because the major security preoccupation of the Cold War, the nuclear stand-off between the two superpowers, has gone, drawing attention to conflict within states, low-level violence and terrorism. Also, the world of power politics is not behaving according to the principles established by the modern state for the exercise of its power. Familiar terms like balance-of-power, sphere of influence and hegemony are no longer useful. The distinction between foreign policy and domestic policy, which led to the unwritten rule that politics stopped at the water's edge, is blurred, as is the distinction between what is public and what is private. The state, which had been the symbol of what was public, is itself no longer certain of its role. It privatises much of what it used to do under the aegis of public enterprise, promoting the values of "choice" and "user pays" while still behaving as if it is entitled to the loyalty of its citizens. In addition, its own future is in doubt. Over a long period, it had confirmed the axiom that "states make war and war makes states". Now internal wars are unmaking states, which are under threat from these interior tensions and also from outside forces seemingly beyond their control.

The political effect of the turbulence is that the elites of the world gain in wealth and sophistication, embracing global and cosmopolitan values, while the mass of people return to traditional values, reverting to older and more trusted forms of identity. They prefer to be with people like themselves, whom they can instinctively trust, rather than with people declared to be their cohorts by abstract authorities, intellectual, political or financial. They turn to family, religion and ethnicity, where they feel they belong, and where they are not obliged to uphold an unfamiliar or uncomfortable view of history and politics or rights and duties that they do not understand. This division between elites and ordinary people creates a dilemma for political leaders, especially in democracies. They want to be on the bandwagon of change but they need also the votes of a reluctant, even recalcitrant, electorate.

It is unfortunate that the leaders of Australia and the United States, at a critical stage in the evolution of the international system, seem unaware of either the complexity or the promise of the contemporary world. John Howard is a sturdily traditional politician, whose heroes are Winston Churchill, Robert Menzies and Don Bradman, all highly admirable, yet out of their element in the swirling turbulence of today. George W. Bush once had the appetites of a swinger, with a taste for entertainment; since becoming a born-again Christian, he has retreated into a comfort zone of abstract nouns and eternal verities. The particular challenge of the contemporary world is that the responses of the past, no matter how worthy, are no longer effective and the morality of religion, while still powerful, has become dangerous.

*

Three factors in the contemporary world deserve closer scrutiny: global capitalism, political Islam and terrorism.

The process of economic "globalisation" that gained pace after the Cold War ended swept the world, subduing and diffusing the power of states. Increased trade and foreign investment created wealth, but the benefits went mainly to those already wealthy. Of the world's six and a half billion people, about a billion improved their living standard, while four billion became stuck in what the World Bank calls low or lower incomes. Nearly three billion people live on under $US2 a day. The number of poor living in developing or transition economies fell, but due to population growth, the number of people living in poverty actually increased. Nor, of course, did the creation of wealth mean creation of satisfaction or contentment. Those who gained wanted more. Those who missed out were resentful. The creation of wealth was in the abstract a benefit to all, but the perception of the relative gains and losses rather than the absolute benefit was what mattered. In addition, there was a whiff of casino equity in the wealth created. In 1995, midway in the post-Cold War era, the combined annual value of global trade and foreign direct investment amounted to only six days' turnover on the foreign exchange markets. At the time, George Soros, who became a billionaire exploiting the fluctuations of the foreign exchange market, recognised that its effect skewed wealth's bounty so badly that he recommended an international institution like the World Bank or the International Monetary Fund to regulate the trillions of dollars circling the world at any moment on the lookout for foreign exchange opportunities.

In the historic stand-off between capital and labour, globalisation was especially partial. Capital could be transferred with the click of a mouse and goods and services were increasingly traded globally, but labour did not have a seat at what was called the "banquet table". Labour was treated as a cost, not as an asset; as workers are not only an integral part of the economic system but also human beings with rights, this brought into play a host of political and social factors not merely economic. As citizens of the state, entitled to its protection, they were, in democracies, also voters. The dynamo of successful capitalism has been that its workers are both producers and consumers, paid enough in the first role to make them effective in the second. The traditional jobs of workers in developed countries disappeared. Workers in developing countries would have liked to be consumers as well as producers, but part of their "comparative advantage" was that their wages were low. The global movement of labour was almost entirely from poor countries to richer countries and became entangled with asylum seekers, sometimes supported by criminal networks set up to evade the authority of the state.

Trade and investment and the financial services necessary to support them, the wealth-creating dynamic of the capitalist system, rode roughshod at times over human concerns and sensibilities. The cautionary tale of the stalled Multilateral Agreement on Investment (MAI) – which would restrict the right of democratically elected governments to regulate currency speculation or give preference to local investment – was evidence of resentment with the "bottom line" demands of global capital. The debacle of the World Trade Organisation meeting in Seattle in December, 1999, and others since, showed resistance to a liberal free-trade agenda by the developing countries and a demand by trade unionists and environmentalists to be at the negotiating table. In the eyes of the more eloquent of those who organised the rebellious demonstration at Seattle, the International Monetary Fund, World Bank and WTO represented an "iron triangle of corporate rule", which was "frog-marching humanity, along with the rest of the planet, into a toxic, money-maddened, repressive future".[1] The state, for all its muscularity when protecting its interests, was weakly compliant when offered money. Democratic states, including Australia, thumbed their noses at United Nations treaty committees dealing in human rights, but collapsed when faced with something like the MAI.

The president of the World Bank, James Wolfensohn, among others, voiced concern that the benefits of globalisation were not reaching the poor. The argument that globalisation is inherently democratic, by forcing governments to be transparent and increasing access to information and new technology, fell flat when most of the world's people did not have that access and, on present trends, were unlikely to get it. Wolfensohn made the point clear: "Technology and its consequences are increasingly linking us together into one world. But this 'one world' cannot remain split along the fault line that separates the lives and aspirations of the rich and the poor. Technological progress alone will not bridge the divide. Rather, our sense of common humanity must be the shared bond."[2]

If recent corporate amalgamations are an indication of things to come, globalisation will return, and with additional force. The economic incentives are powerful and the political and cultural effects irresistible. In the years 1995–2000, 344 new embassies were established (only a few countries experienced a decline in the number of embassies they hosted) and 342 new memberships in international organisations were recorded. The huge television audiences for soccer and rugby world competitions are a reminder that globalisation can draw on local cultures that do not share American values, at least in football. It is both a liberalising, indeed liberating, force, so that in order to deal with it successfully, governments will need to be more transparent and accountable and it is also, on the other side of its coinage, an anti-democratic force, overwhelming local authenticity, countermanding, in the pursuit of markets, the freedom of people to choose through the ballot box governments that express their will. The important debate about how to use the creative force of globalisation while treating its pathological tendencies was interrupted by the war on terrorism and needs to be resumed.

⋆

American dominance, riding the turbulence when the Cold War ended, prodded an already restless and resurgent Islam. The youngest of the world's major religions, Islam has had a chequered political history, rising to heights during the Ottoman Empire, when from its base in Turkey it controlled at one stage Egypt, Syria, Crete, Greece, the Balkans, Hungary, the Caucasus and Persia. Its influence spread as far as Morocco and Spain in the west, to north and central Africa and, in the east, to central, south and south-east Asia as far as Indonesia. With more than a billion followers (and a high birth rate, expected to raise the figure to 1.9 billion by 2020), Islam today has about the same population as China or India, not concentrated within one nation-state, however, but widely spread. No great power or combination of powers promotes Islam.

Its people and territory were colonised by the Europeans, who took over additional territory from Turkey after the First World War. The Arabs were promised much by the British and the French, but what they got after the Second World War was Israel, a source of anger and frustration ever since. They found, when the French and British withdrew, that the Americans were no more understanding. At the time of the Suez crisis, 1956, the Americans seemed prepared to show sympathy, against the wishes of the British, French and Israelis, for the action of Egypt's leader Gamal Abdel Nasser in nationalising the Anglo-French company that ran the canal. It was an attempt to straddle support for Israel and encouragement for a group of young Arab reformers like Nasser who were emerging as political leaders in the Middle East. This was at a time when the Americans were engaged in rivalry with the Europeans over the conduct of the Cold War and when Washington was contemplating the value of Islam as an ally against Godless communism.

One of the al Qaeda leaders who became close to Osama bin Laden was a young doctor in Cairo when Nasser came to power. He was a member of the Brotherhood, a militant group that opposed Nasser on the grounds that his model for Egypt's development was Turkey, a secular state that corrupted the Islamic ideal. An intense debate within Islam about the relationship between religion and state continues to this day. How a band of fanatical Muslims who saw themselves as martyrs willing to die if necessary for the faith, defined themselves in terms of anti-accommodation, even hostility, to everything Western, especially American, is a story beyond the scope of this book. But two brief comments can be made.

Islam awaits its Reformation. It has not been successful in adapting in the modern world to the rise of the secular state and its tentacular agents, democracy and capitalism. While Confucian states have generally succeeded with capitalism, and are grappling with democracy, and Hindu India has adopted both, Islamic states have been trapped in dynastic political structures and a debilitating argument about the relationship between mosque and state. Islam's great days were in the feudal era, with hierarchical political structures and a powerful military. Some contemporary Muslim states are rich, because of natural resources, but their societies are brittle. A high birth rate is filling the streets with youth without prospects. Hence, there is a violent quality about the resurgence of Islam, conveyed not just in the destruction of capitalism's skyscraper but, in another arresting image, the demolition of the giant Buddha statues in Afghanistan.

Saudi Arabia is perhaps the least attractive, according to American values, of the US's Arab allies, being governed by a ubiquitous monarchy, dependent on oil and tourism and sustained by an economy that requires foreign workers and experts to run it. As the birthplace of the prophet Muhammad, it is both a source of the frustration that the Islamic jihadists feel and a source also of some of their substantial funds. At times, states as varied as Libya, Iran and Syria have threatened to form an anti-American bloc. The well-established rift between Sunnis and Shiites no longer explains attitudes to the West; the division is now between reformers, hamstrung by a record of failure in accommodation with the West, and purists, who maintain that only the true faith will deliver social and economic justice. Neither supports the terrorists, although at times each seems to be half in sympathy with them.

The second comment is a reminder that there was a power vacuum when the Cold War ended. A new disposition of power did not emerge, and still hasn't. The United States was head and shoulders above all others, no other country, or combination of countries, could check or counter it. With globalisation, it seemed to be surfing a wave of strategic, economic, political and cultural power that could not be stopped. Islam, already at a disadvantage in a world dominated by Western ideas of the secular state, democracy and capitalism, had no alternative sources of power now to which it could turn. The communist states were in disarray. The non-aligned bloc had lost its role. For the purists, it seemed that all that could save Muslims from being drowned in a sea of Western modernism was the religion itself.

⋆

Terrorism was also an unwelcome dividend of the Cold War peace. Long before September 11, 2001, terrorism had become a prominent item on the international agenda, although there was no agreed definition of it. One person's terrorist was another's freedom fighter. There was cyber terrorism, which could be highly disruptive but was not violent. There was random terrorism, which was violent but without a political objective. State terrorism was both violent and political, but its existence was clouded by official dissembling. Practised noticeably in some Muslim states, such as Iran, Libya and Iraq, and in communist North Korea, it was also the secret weapon of Western intelligence and counter-intelligence agencies, including the Central Intelligence Agency of the United States.

Spectacular events like the Sarin nerve gas attack in the Tokyo subway by the Aum Shinrikyo sect in 1995, the destruction of the Oklahoma federal government building with home-made bombs in 1995 and the bombing of the US embassies in Kenya and Tanzania in 1998 created media waves but did not indicate the extent and depth of terrorism as a serious international problem. The evidence showed an increase in frequency and lethal efficiency. Three explanations were common: ethno-nationalism and separatism, Islamic fundamentalism and the emergence of *ad-hoc* terrorism. A rise in militant activity occurred across fundamentalist and extremist organisations – messianic Zionists, underground Christian sects in the United States, radical Hindu and Sikh groups in India, millenarian cults in Europe, North America and Japan. Wanton acts of death and destruction in the pursuit of "evil" – in the form of apostates, demons of disorder and other opponents of holy causes – grew more frequent.

Weapon stocks left over from the Cold War were a

factor. A wide range of weaponry became available – not just rifles and machine-guns, but land mines, rocket-propelled grenades and shoulder-launched surface-to-air missiles. Some areas, such as South Asia, were awash with arms after the withdrawal of Russia from Afghanistan. Parts of southern Africa, Cambodia, Russia and Eastern Europe became active trading regions. Arms exports to sub-Saharan Africa rose spectacularly. The question arose whether terrorists might resort to weapons of mass destruction. Chemical and biological agents were more easily available. The technical expertise to construct a nuclear bomb was available on the internet or from Russian experts desperate to supplement their incomes.

Terrorism, like crime and poverty, has always been with us. In hierarchical systems, assassination of the monarch, the emperor or sultan was a preferred option, on the theory that, if the head was severed, the body ceased to function. The spread of democracy countered this tendency. The system became flexible; it adapted and continued. If leaders were elected, their successors could also be elected. Similarly, with democracy came bureaucracy. The institutions of the state, the armed forces, the law courts, the treasury, the police, were no longer the personal property of the head of state, and they too could adapt to the removal of a head of state or of a government or a minister or an important official. Terrorists began to broaden their attack, killing civilians, including children, in the hope of putting pressure on the society and through it the government. Modern terrorism prefers these so-called "soft" targets to the "hard" targets of the official state and its representatives, army depots, embassies and official buildings, although both strategies continue. The soft targets are obviously more difficult to defend. And in trying to defend them the state has to concede ground to the terrorists by restricting the freedoms which the civilian population wants to continue to enjoy.

What creates a terrorist, as distinct from an activist, is a subject too big to be tackled here, but it can be said that terrorists often exist not because they are inherently bad people but because they are powerless to right some wrong they wish, however improbably, to correct. Terrorism is a weapon of the weak. Powerful organisations and states may use it from time to time, but it is incidental to their strategies in the main game, whose rules they have made or at least accept. Terrorists operate outside the rules, which are by definition, according to them, unfair. They are an irritant rather than a rival of the main players. The strategy of terrorism is to terrorise, to unbalance stronger opponents by scaring them. Whether a terrorist campaign is successful depends on the reaction of its targets. The considerable literature of counter-terrorism has a single message. Deny the terrorists oxygen. Don't give them publicity.

The issue that arises with the 2003 invasion of Iraq is whether this is the right way to counter terrorism.

Regimented Iraq was not a fertile source for the terrorists who planned the attack on the World Trade Center and the Pentagon. They came from Egypt, Jordan, Saudi Arabia and Yemen. Their funds were raised, not from Iraq, but from wealthy sympathisers and charities, especially in Saudi Arabia, and laundered in freewheeling financial hubs like Dubai.

Declaring war, turning a weak opponent into a fearsome enemy, runs contrary to the lesson of history. Even with advances in technology, especially in weapons of mass destruction, the core of terrorism is unchanged. It avoids confrontation, relying on hit-and-run tactics with dramatic effect. In this respect, al Qaeda is no different. It has refined one of the most enduring of the secrets of espionage, which is that resentment is the most fertile ground for recruitment, but that is not new. What is new is its use of the computer and the internet. Its technical knowledge and skill at networking, recruiting and fund-raising also have an international reach more powerful than terrorist organisations of the past. It is also insatiable, in the sense that it is impossible to imagine how any of its proclaimed objectives (like the destruction of the United States or the end of Western civilisation) can be achieved, although these are more likely cover for more precise objectives, such as the replacement of secular Muslim states, like Turkey, or sycophantic Muslim states, like Saudi Arabia, with Islamist states more like Iran.

The call to war, while it may have political satisfaction, is actually confusing, because, although terrorism cannot "win", it cannot be "defeated" either. Terrorism is a clumsy weapon, reached for in desperation. It antagonises the public and galvanises the powerful. But it can wear a society down, fray its spirit. If it is a blunt, pathetic weapon, so is war. Terrorists want disorder and counter-terrorism must maintain order. A war strategy to counter terrorism is a bull in a china shop. It brings disorder, which is exactly what the terrorist wants. It is counter-productive. It creates terrorists.

★

Beneath the turbulent surface of the contemporary world, a form of order was emerging before the terrorists struck and the United States responded.

International conventions, such as legally enforceable responses to war crimes and crimes against humanity, as well as drug trafficking, disease control and a host of other human activities that are universally seen as either criminal or dangerous, were at the forefront of diplomacy after the Cold War. So too was the construction of frameworks that would enable states to pool their resources in dealing with less obvious, yet perhaps more damaging long-term dangers from climate change and unbalanced demography. In the middle of the decade it was estimated that some 50,000 international "instruments" of various kinds existed, with some 2000 inter-governmental agencies to put them into effect.

There were 920 treaties in force for Australia, and about 7000 in force for the United States.

Intervention on humanitarian grounds in Rwanda and Somalia, while less than successful, was prompted by a growing view that the boundaries of sovereign states should not protect the destruction of people and property. In the former Yugoslavia, both the United Nations and NATO intervened and the former Serbian head of state, Slobodan Milosevic, found himself facing 61 charges before a United Nations tribunal for war crimes and crimes against humanity at The Hague. Chile's head of state, Augusto Pinochet, was trapped on a visit to London for medical reasons by the Convention Against Torture, which both Britain and Chile had ratified. What was called a "truth and reconciliation" process was established in some Latin American countries and in South Africa, where both violators and victims of violations of human rights were encouraged to tell the truth. The International Criminal Court which, unlike the International Court of Justice, will try not only states but individuals as well, was established.

Milosevic could point to his domestic support, even from political opponents. He could claim that he acted to protect the survival of the state, not to mention Serbian, or even European, culture. He could argue that the Kosovo Liberation Army was a Muslim terrorist group that needed to be suppressed so that law and order could be restored. Pinochet could say that he had saved Chile from collapse and had rebuilt its economy.

He had stepped down when the people voted against him. He may have been a dictator, but he was a successful one, handing back his country in good shape to a properly elected successor. Yet both their claims on behalf of the state were rejected, one by the processes of international law and convention and the other by the decisions of the United Nations and the world's most powerful military alliance, NATO.

During this run of active internationalism, Australia experienced a golden period and the United States, while it had reservations about rules that protected the weak as well as the strong, was usually able – more successfully than Russia or China – to be active in the United Nations and international organisations. The most negative effect of our current alliance strategy is that it takes no account of what has been slowly emerging as an alternative to world order based on military power.

In essence, the alternative order gives international expression to the concept of the rule of law. It is based on the multilateral system, including organisations as diverse as the World Bank, the World Trade Organisation, the International Maritime Organisation, the International Atomic Energy Agency, the United Nations High Commission for Refugees and, recently, the International Criminal Court. It reflects the evolution of the international system of states from a primitive form in which peace is established by the use of power, usually by going to war, to one where security resides in mutually beneficial arrangements that are reached by agreement.

The process is slow and intermittent, as you would expect. The rules are not yet fully understood or obeyed. The nation-state still maintains its sovereign independence. Some states accept regulatory power in advance of their actions, others prefer freedom to act with consequences to be determined afterwards. On security issues, a critical mass has not yet been reached. When it does, it will need underpinning. For the rule of law to be obeyed, there needs to be law enforcement. Within states, the state itself has a monopoly. It makes the law and enforces it, but globally there is no such law enforcement. The United Nations has no such monopoly, either to legislate or to enforce. It relies on the resources of its members, who are sovereign states, and who sometimes, if they are powerful enough, ignore it.

So what should we do? Behave as if we are living in a world where law and order are actually enforced by powerful states, or in a world where law and order might in the future be established by international co-operation and enforced by an international regime? In this period of transition, most people and most states will prudently depend on the balance of order and freedom that their own countries can provide. In particular, they will ensure that they can defend themselves and that they are equipped to counter terrorism. But those states and peoples with an eye to the future will give support when they can to the emerging international order. It is the great issue of political leadership and statecraft in this century, and it is unfortunate that political leaders in the United States and Australia at this moment do not seem aware of it or, if they are, seem determined to ignore it or even to defy it.

COSMIC AVENGER

American isolationism can be described politely as a myth. It was created by the first president, George Washington, in the flush of revolutionary independence, when he warned his country against "entangling alliances" in Europe. It is kept alive at home by a streak of sentiment that values everything American and is suspicious of everything foreign and, outside the country, by allies, especially Britain and Australia, who worry that, when they are threatened, the Americans will not come to their aid. But from an historical perspective, American behaviour is not isolationist at all: it is actually a unilateral or solitary form of interventionism.

When they declared their independence from the British in 1776, the Americans were a nation of about four million people inhabiting an eastern coastal strip. They spread across the continent, justifying expansion by their "manifest destiny" to occupy the land from "sea to shining sea", bringing them into conflict with the native populations, the French, the Spanish and the Mexicans. The Monroe Doctrine in 1823 kept foreigners out of the American hemisphere, not to protect the countries of Latin and Central America from intervention but to reserve it for the United States. In the rest of the world, the US has been isolationist only in the sense that it has been reluctant to intervene in conflicts defined by someone else. So it was hesitant in both the First World War and the Second World War, but when it can define the terms, the US readily intervenes, not just to protect its own territory but also in the defence of interests beyond its shores. It has done so frequently in Central and Latin America, for example in Cuba, Dominican Republic, Grenada, Guatemala, Haiti, Mexico, Nicaragua and Panama, where in 1989 its invasion force killed 550 people, arrested the president Manuel Noriega, who had been at one time a favourite of the Central Intelligence Agency, and transported him to the United States for trial in an American court. It tried several times to "eliminate" Juan Peron in Argentina during and after the Second World War. Its attempts to kill Fidel Castro are almost legendary. In the nineteenth and early twentieth century its forces turned up in Japan and China in pursuit of commercial interests. It even became a colonial power in the Pacific, taking the Philippines as a trophy of war with Spain.

Put simply, the United States has been effective in exploiting the opportunities abroad that its successful and highly geared economy created, by using its political and military muscle to protect these commercial outposts. A little known book, *The Influence of Sea*

Power upon History 1660–1783 by Captain Alfred Mahan, published in 1890, is still a valuable guide to the way the United States operates in the world. Mahan's message to his fellow Americans then was that the desirable expansion of American commerce world-wide, which they all supported, needed a strong navy with fuelling posts and bases around the world from which it could police these markets. Today, his language is archaic but his message still resonates.

In 1941, Henry Luce claimed the twentieth century as America's own. "It now becomes our time to be the powerhouse from which the ideals spread throughout the world and do their mysterious work of lifting the life of mankind from the level of beasts to what the Psalmist called a little lower than the angels." He was right about the twentieth century being America's. What about the twenty-first?

Was the twentieth century, violent and restless, creative and destructive, particularly suited to the United States? Will the twenty-first century be different, so different that, unless the United States changes, it will not be as dominant at the end of the century as it is now? In the light of the way American power is currently being tested, this is an important question for those, like Australia, who have invested greatly for their future in a military alliance with the United States. The invasion of Iraq has become the catalyst of a debate about the United States and the way it uses its power. The intervention was conceived and managed in a way that raised questions about the competence of the Bush administration and tensions between its leading members. It appeared at times to have become dysfunctional, and neither the President nor his national security adviser, Dr Condoleezza Rice, seemed to have the temperament or the skill to pull the team together. But the bigger question in the debate is not related to the difficulties of the mission, painful as this may be for all involved, but what it tells the world about the way the United States exerts its power.

The debate will continue whatever the result in Iraq because it is not just a debate about Iraq, nor the Middle East, nor even terrorism, but about the United States of America. For Americans who want to believe they are pursuing a noble cause in Iraq – the most important foreign policy initiative by the United States so far this century – the purpose of this book is to post a traffic warning: Wrong Way – Go Back. Or, perhaps, in the manner of one of Mr Luce's publications, "Little lower than angels not yet status of US in mysterious anti-beast campaign."

*

When the twentieth century dawned the United States was a minor player in world politics. At the turn of the twenty-first century it stood head and shoulders above all others.

It was the world's greatest producer and greatest consumer, possessing about 30 per cent of total world product. It spent 36 per cent of the global military budget (since increased). It had been on the winning side in the First World War and the Second World War and had led the West to victory in the Cold War, so its political authority was unrivalled. In addition, its popular culture was adopted everywhere, including in former communist countries, especially Russia, where it was chic. Everyone, or almost everyone, said "Have a Nice Day". A host in south-east Asia, after a day complaining that his country's culture was being undermined, surprised at a karaoke bar in the evening with a heartfelt impersonation of Frank Sinatra singing "My Way". The US was streets ahead of others in the number of Nobel Prize laureates and in gold medallists at the Olympic Games. And it invented the internet.

The United States is still on a rising trajectory. It is not a mature power, ripe or ready for decline. Its current supremacy may last for some time, but it is based on being exceptional rather than dominant. The US in its current mood does not regard itself as a nation-state, like everyone else, with interests and ideas that can be negotiated and discussed in the global marketplace. It regards itself rather as a model for others to follow. If they resist, the explanation can only lie in their ignorance or their malevolence, because the US has shown from its own experience that it has the secret of how to be peaceful and prosperous. This attitude makes it awkward in leadership roles, even when it is competent in what it sets out to do and even when the values for which it stands are those that serve the progression of civilisation.

The terrorist attacks on September 11 revived an aspect of the United States that admirers of its liberal democracy had hoped, with the end of the Cold War, had receded. Frequent presidential references to the "greatest nation on earth" jarred on foreign ears, whatever their local reception. There was an element of old-fashioned morality and revenge – an eye for an eye – in the US response. Baying for blood, over-riding the views and experiences of others in a burst of nationalism, patriotism, self-righteousness and frontier morality alerted non-Americans to a mood swing between anger and petulance. Osama bin Laden became a spectre haunting America, as if capturing or killing him would remove, like the spider from its web, the source of trouble. There was also an echo of Cold War confusion, when it was not clear whether the war was against communism everywhere and anywhere or against those powers, especially the Soviet Union, that supported it. This kind of rhetoric over-rides the realism of international relations, as it has always done in the United States.

There is a harshness about the United States which is an amalgam of several things – a belief in good and evil, in facts and literal meanings, in efficiency and outcomes, in the power of numbers, especially money, as well as in justice and equity. One can admire a country for its energy and its productivity, its efficiency and physical beauty, its determination to be ruled by law and not by people, without discovering any innate charm. America, and therefore Americans, can seem overbearing at times, as if the world in which they live is controlled and predictable and they know only too well how it works. The range of variety, ambiguity, mystery and contingency, which the rest of the world exhibits in abundance, while sometimes irritating, can also be charming and exciting. For Americans it is an existence of inferior quality and potential danger. Their determination to strive and reward, to pass on knowledge and leave their world, and in particular the United States, a better place for their brief existence in it can be moving and inspiring. It can also be dramatic. But it is not often surprising.

Until it put its stamp on the Cold War, the United States was not taken seriously by non-Americans as a political, cultural or intellectual source of modern civilisation. It was the centre of Know-How and Can-Do, the factory of the world, the capital of labour-saving devices and other marvellous gadgetry, the home of comics and action movies. It was also known – and laughed at – for its upward social mobility, so that all Americans who were not millionaires were believed to consider themselves to be middle class. Side by side with brutal social attitudes, as shown in the treatment of African-Americans, was the solemn language of respectability. The fruitologist emerged from the greengrocer, the lubritorium from the petrol station and "my son, the doctor" became, even for Americans, a figure of fun.

Jacques Barzun complained about lack of style in America. Henry James thought what he called "items of high civilisation" were absent. Realism and naturalism in the novel, pragmatism in philosophy, scientific and technological exploration in industry and a lack of interest in scholarship and jurisprudence were dominant. James was not the most sympathetic observer of his native country, but he was probably right. Life moved so fast that any commentary on it was likely to be out of date by the time it was made. Real life was making money and conquering a continent and, although artists and thinkers tried to grapple with high civilisation, one item of which in James' mind was moral purpose, they were just as excited by what was going on around them as was everyone else. They didn't necessarily admire it, or even like it, but they couldn't help being fascinated by it.

Americans are caught between two worlds. They are not an old civilisation, in which lack of surprise might be explained by weariness or the weight of knowing that there is nothing new under the sun. But neither is the United States any more a new society, in which the mistakes of adolescence have their own tender appeal. The United States is now a great and powerful cultural force; its public debates overflow its boundaries. Freedom of speech and assembly, abortion, gun control, capital punishment, public accountability – issues like these are debated by Americans with a harsh vigour, secure in their history and their constitutional guarantees. But when the debate overflows into the world, the contending positions seem to outsiders sometimes to lack maturity, or human sensitivity.

The United States is not naturally an orderly, stable society in which what is odd or unknown can be glimpsed without alarm. What is odd or unknown is either a threat, which needs to be countered, or an event, which can be exploited. The United States is a disorderly and volatile society. It keeps itself orderly by allowing the conflicts which are inherent in an open society to check and balance themselves while, like most societies, using the law and its enforcement agencies to keep the surface as smooth as possible. This produces extreme contention, which is satisfied because it is not repressed, not because it resolves anything.

The extensive debate of issues in the United States and their extension beyond its borders through American command of information technology has led to an impression that America is a multi-faceted little universe, not a country. You can find evidence in some part of it of whatever it is you are seeking. Yet it has made its mark on the world by being American. What non-Americans have noticed and admired about the United States, or sometimes disliked, has been its American quality. The crucial difference with Europe is that the individual European states, now being melded into some kind of a union, are deeply steeped in history.

The United States in history is America itself. Although its size and dramatic geography have created regions with different attributes and achievements, its contribution to history since its beginning has been as the explorer of territory previously unmarked, the conqueror of peoples previously unknown and the creator of a way of life previously unimagined, which in the twentieth century has been called "modern" and which has spread throughout the world. The genius of Americans is that, in inventing the future for themselves, they have discovered that it is the future that most of the rest of the people of the world also want, although they would like to say that they discovered it for themselves.

During the Cold War, the communist states, especially the Soviet Union, raised the flag of the traditional arts, while the United States exported what was modern. The Soviet Union made a point of preserving the classics. It was a surprise to those who had expected that a revolutionary government would have preferred revolutionary arts, but the Soviet leaders realised early that revolutionary art was exactly what they did not want. Artists were temperamental and egocentric enough, without being revolutionary as well. They also found that their artists, especially in ballet, were generally delighted to be patronised by the state. Bolshoi diplomacy – like badminton diplomacy for the Chinese – became a feature of Soviet efforts to establish itself as an equal contender with the United States on the world's stage. The United States exported contemporary dance rather than classical ballet, and jazz, musicals and popular singers rather than opera and classical music. Also, to combat racial criticism, they included many black performers.

With film and jazz, America chose its strengths. It is the fountainhead, the source, without which it is hard to imagine the existence of these two great arts of the twentieth century. Each began elsewhere: film in France with the Lumiere brothers and jazz in Africa, then to the cotton fields of the American South. It was in America, however, that they took hold, were shaped and presented to the world. They have something in common. They are contemporary, they are essentially populist and they are unpretentious – that is, they are not pure. They take from anywhere and give to anyone.

My own introduction to America was in my first serious job, as a film critic for a daily newspaper. For a period of about five years, I saw hundreds, perhaps even thousands of films, most of which were American. Many were awful; most were entertaining, some were absorbing, compelling, moving; a few were magnificent. I liked the energy of American films, the way they got on with the business of telling a story, their inventiveness and, in comparison with British and European films, their pervasive democratic values. But perhaps more than anything American films gave a properly brought-up Australian a foretaste of the potential for horrible behaviour in human beings. The Hollywood moral code that encouraged patriotism and prohibited sexual licence did not prevent violence, and Hollywood knew that violent action was entertaining. The effect on film and television viewers is often debated, but we have learned like everyone else that human beings can be more cruel and violent to each other than even Hollywood could imagine. What humans have done to other humans down the ages, and recently in Croatia, Bosnia, Kosovo, Somalia, Rwanda, East Timor, Afghanistan and Iraq, just to mention a few, has nothing to do with the influence of violent film and television fare.

★

America's two staples of freedom – democracy as a form of checks and balances against the power of the state, and capitalism as private ownership of resources competing in an open market – combine in a recipe for nation-building that has worked with great effect for Americans, making the United States the richest and most powerful state the world has seen, but its influence as a model for others has been spotty. Minimal government, leaving the people's social, economic and cultural needs to be met by the private sector, is not an attractive model for developing countries, where the state has newly acquired power and the private sector is weak. Even in developed countries, the American political model, with its complex internal dynamics and built-in tendency to expose itself to the media, is copied with caution. The architecture of government is so complex in Washington that if one institution decides, another checks or counters. George Schultz, former secretary of state, once remarked that there was no such thing as a final decision in Washington.

The presidential system, with the chief executive chosen by popular vote, is more easily transplanted, attracting sometimes, however, celebrities and personalities who promise much and are unable to deliver. Even at home, the presidential voting system has weaknesses. The cost of running for public office in the United States, especially for the presidency, has become so daunting that only those already rich or capable of raising corporate-size campaign war chests are deemed to be eligible. For a large, cosmopolitan, multi-racial, multi-cultural and multi-religious society, the US has delivered to the White House a remarkably bland version of political leadership, favouring rich men and military leaders, failing to elect a Catholic until 1960 and, even now, a woman or a Jew.

The message of unremitting success that the American model promotes as economic and social progress is also, while dazzling, limited in its appeal. Most people in the world live in "quiet desperation", as Henry David Thoreau, an American writer who defied American values, once said about his own neighbourhood. The civic virtue of Americans contains little wisdom, except wise-cracking humour or perhaps a lecture on self-improvement, for those who are failures in the money-making system it promotes. Globalisation brought to the surface American impatience with slow and inefficient societies and smothered within the United States emotional sympathy for the poor and underprivileged of the world that was evident during earlier presidencies, such as Franklin Roosevelt's, when the Great Depression exposed a severe shortage in the system's bounty. Most of the world's people are poor. The energy and optimism of America is of value to them, as is its remarkable confidence, as the Can-Do country *par excellence,* that no task is beyond it. The poor of the world need assistance from those who are successful. Still, the high-wire performance of Wall Street, which holds Americans and many in other advanced economies in thrall, is fantasy land to most people. Societies that are strong and confident in themselves can sometimes incorporate the American model of success without losing their own sense of direction, but societies that are finding their way in the world risk being enthralled or alternatively repelled by it.

Democracy and the market economy have been slow to take root in the United States' own backyard, Central and Latin America. In Chile, where democracy was stronger than elsewhere in the hemisphere, the US role in the overthrow of President Allende and support of General Pinochet was reactionary. A century ago it helped the Cubans to throw off the Spanish, but for the last half-century or so has been at loggerheads with the island state. Its influence in Haiti waxes and wanes without discernible effect on the politics or living standard of a deeply impoverished and troubled people. Mexico's troubled relationship with its huge neighbour is improving under the influence of the North American Free Trade Agreement (NAFTA) but is still less than friendly.

In Asia, the success story is Japan. An intense, nationalistic and martial society has become, under American influence, a global economic power and a stable democracy, perhaps too stable, as there has been only one change of government – and for a short period – from the conservative political alliance that has ruled since the Americans forced Japan to become a democracy after the Second World War. The US has not had a close relationship with the world's most populous democracy, India, although it has had a close relationship with neighbouring Pakistan, where democracy languishes and the army and military intelligence seem to have a perpetual option on government. It is committed to the defence of Taiwan, which limits its influence with the region's growing power, China. Its relations with South Korea are strong, but in unusual circumstances: unlike Germany, Korea remains divided, a relic of the Cold War. Since the war with Vietnam, American influence in south-east Asia has, if anything, declined, although it retained links with the army in Indonesia.

In the Middle East, one-sided support for Israel has undermined its influence. Democracy and the free market has not a high US priority, but access to fuel has. The efficiency of the American economy, and consequently the high living standards of Americans, depends on supplies of cheap oil and gas. So the US has business relationships with Arab states, without being able to make headway with its political and moral message. In sub-Saharan Africa, the US has lost influence since the Cold War. The movement for African Union is looking more to Europe than to the United States for inspiration.

*

US foreign policy is submerged in the language of morality. The first white Americans came from Europe to escape religious persecution, and the American outlook still reflects that initial concern with liberty. Like all national outlooks, it is flawed by human nature. When they declared that all men are created equal, with the same unalienable rights to life, liberty and the pursuit of happiness, the early Americans were asserting equality with their former overlords, the British, not with the Africans who had been brought to America to labour in the plantations as slaves. Australians are similarly human. The first white Australians were transported across the world because the gaols in Britain were at bursting point, and our outlook still reflects an abiding concern with social and economic conditions. Our egalitarian ethos, a form of revolt against the British, did not prevent us, however, from adopting a racist immigration policy and adopting British cultural styles and aristocratic forms of social recognition.

Foreign policy attracts moral rhetoric probably because the interests it promotes are so obviously pragmatic. The Europeans colonised most of the world with promises of progress. The Czars evoked Christianity to create an empire that became the Soviet Union. American foreign policy is more honest than most; it gives moral value to its national interests by claiming that the United States is engaged in a crusade against evil. If there is evil in the world, it is the duty of Americans to find it and stamp it out. The evil is almost always discerned as a form of tyranny, bad government over good people. The current axis of evil – Iraq, Iran and North Korea – combines three vastly different forms of tyranny, a dictatorship before the fall of Saddam Hussein, an Islamic autocracy and a communist regime, but the core of evil is the same. The people are not "free".

It is a powerful message that engages the American people in foreign policy. Specialists often complain that US foreign policy is driven by American domestic politics and there is substance in the complaint. The commercial drive is powerful and there is hidden anxiety about a moral universe, conveyed in Frances Fitzgerald's evocative phrase, that Americans relate "the fall of sparrows in distant lands to some fault or virtue in American policy". On the other hand, popular engagement means that foreign policy is not cocooned away by professionals as too esoteric, complex and politically sensitive to be aired in public.

Moral engagement is also part of the American media's determination to root out corruption in high places, no matter what the effect on patriotic sentiment in time of war. American journalism takes its public role seriously. "Embedded" in the ranks of the military during the initial invasion of Iraq, the US media was subdued, but it is again on a mission to expose corrupt behaviour over the use of torture and the misuse of intelligence. Perhaps the most celebrated case was the printing of the *Pentagon Papers* by the *New York Times* in 1971. A massive (3000 pages) documentation of American involvement in Indo-China, including the Vietnam War, compiled by the Pentagon over a year and a half, the *Pentagon Papers* showed the gap between what the US government actually did, and was doing, in Vietnam and what it told the American people. After the first instalments, the *New York Times* was taken to court by the Justice Department on the reasonable grounds that the nation was at war and printing a top-secret document was harmful to its national defence interests.

Justice Hugo Black's judgment in favour of the *New York Times* read, in part:

> Only a free and unrestrained press can effectively expose deception in government. And paramount among the responsibilities of a free press is the duty to prevent any part of the Government from deceiving the people and sending them off to distant lands to die of foreign fevers and foreign shot and shell.

> In my view, far from deserving condemnation for their courageous reporting, the *New York Times*, the *Washington Post* and other newspapers should be commended for serving the purpose that the Founding Fathers saw so clearly. In revealing the workings of government that led to the Vietnam War, the newspapers nobly did precisely that which the founders hoped and trusted they would do.[3]

It is difficult to imagine any other judiciary in the world making such a judgment. Constitutional backing gives the American media legal protection to stand against governments and to expose powerful forces and institutions, even when the state can claim that it is at war and vital national interests are at stake. Similarly the US Supreme Court's rejection in July 2004 of executive privilege in relation to prisoners held in Guantanamo Bay was an assertion of separate power that would have been breathtaking in most countries, and in terror-stricken America was a breath of fresh air.

There is something entirely admirable about the American determination to get at the truth, whatever the fall-out, and I have never been able to understand the view that American democracy is some kind of conspiracy to create consensus for the status quo. It is another myth that will not go away, like the misconception that because of the overwhelming influence of business, the constraints on government and the absence of a party of reform, the US is a conservative society. In fact, from another perspective, the United States is a radical society. During a century in which governments have not just been strong but overpowering, the US rose to the top while emphasising weak government, strong individuals and a strong civil society. In its constitutional protection of the individual against the state, the US is the most radical society in the world. It even provides legal support for citizens to bear arms without the authority of the state – indeed, some believe, against their own state.

This does not make the United States any easier to live with, nor to work with; the experience of engaging with the United States can be unsettling. As the racist nationalists of South Africa and the reforming communists of the Soviet Union discovered, American involvement in your affairs can be subversive, undermining the position from which you thought you were negotiating. This is because the United States is not just a nation with national interests which can be satisfied by give and take, although it has such interests and it knows how to cut a deal. It is also driven by values which it believes are not only responsible for its own creation, and are therefore self-evidently effective, but are also universal, making it a duty to share them with other people and other states.

It is a compelling idea. For politicians, not just American, it is almost irresistible. It is a call for "leadership". The dreary business of massaging the constituencies, listening to all the public – and private – voices, keeping an eye on the numbers, calibrating the national interest, dodging the snipers in the opinion pages and smiling for the media are suddenly replaced by a single stance and a single message, with a pedestal underfoot. And it resonates with the public, even when it happens not to be the right statecraft to counter terrorism.

What gives Americans much of their moral and indeed physical energy is what prevents them from co-operating with other states. Americans believe that the system they have devised for themselves is the source of their greatness. Other systems, no matter how efficient or idealistic, fall short. The combination of unilateralism in behaviour and self-regard or, what is known as American "exceptionalism", makes it hard for the United States to co-operate with other states on an equal footing, or for other states to co-operate with them. The Americans are always tempted by the argument that they can decide on their own the terms of agreement or, if necessary, disagreement. For allies, as Australia is now discovering, this attitude does not leave much room to move.

American righteousness may be palatable for those who share its values or who need American protection, but it is a persistent source of anxiety for those who do not. Some Americans rationalise this by using the formula that "those who are not for us are against us." This only deepens the anxiety, because it is obvious that these Americans cannot comprehend values other than their own. In this sense, some anti-Americanism is self-inflicted. The highly regarded speech of President George W. Bush to Congress nine days after the terrorist attack expressed a view of the world understandingly simplified by America's grief and anger, but nevertheless concerning for any government or people with its own experience of terrorism.

> Our war on terror begins with al Qaeda, but it does not end there. It will not end until every terrorist group of global reach has been found, stopped and defeated … Every nation, in every region, now has a decision to make. Either you are with us, or you are with the terrorists. From this day forward, any nation that continues to harbour or support terrorism will be regarded by the United States as a hostile regime.[4]

This was the speech of an American president who was taking over, like it or not. This was the same rhetoric as that famously used during the Cold War by the Secretary of State, John Foster Dulles, who declared to the non-aligned states that neutrality in the contest between the United States (good) and the Soviet Union (evil) was immoral.

Anti-Americanism is partly a reaction against a preponderance of power and excellence, but it is also a reaction against the attitude behind the power. The high self-regard of Americans can become a danger to themselves. There were warning signs of resistance to

American values long before the terrorist assaults on its territory in 2001. At a 1997 Harvard conference, the elites of countries comprising two-thirds of the world's people – Chinese, Russians, Indians, Arabs, Muslims and Africans – saw the United States as the single greatest external threat to their societies. They did not regard it as a military threat, but as "a menace to their integrity, autonomy, prosperity and freedom of action".[5] Caught up in its own mythology, the US can be its own worst enemy.

POWER AND ORDER

The United States emerged from the Cold War as the only country with a global reach in all forms of power, hard (or coercive) and soft (or persuasive), but nevertheless in economic disarray. It was in no position, except by asking the American public to accept more restraint, to assert its pre-eminence in tangible forms of global political leadership, especially in policing the violence that erupted after the Cold War ended. Rather it rode the surge of globalisation, as the Clinton administration got the economy moving again. The restless, creative energy of a world driven by global economic forces was the reflection writ large of America itself.

When the Cold War ended, the discipline of gearing for war was happily discarded, liberty of opportunity taking over from equality of sacrifice. Democracy and capitalism were now triumphant and no alternative was in sight. Even surviving communist regimes, like China and Vietnam, paid their respects to capitalism, if not to democracy. It was hardly surprising that those elders of society responsible for what had to be endured during a half-century of war should no longer be seen as authoritative figures. A new generation of leaders who had not fought in the Second World War or had not even been prominent during the Cold War was sought, not just because they were free of the baggage of the ideological and cultural wars but because they were more likely to be open to new tests and opportunities. On the left of politics in Western democracies, political differences were submerged in a move to manage, even to manipulate, a fragmented and confused constituency. The successes of Clinton Democrats in the United States, Blair Labour in the United Kingdom and Schroeder Social Democrats in Germany were the result of following what was called "triangular" politics in America, the "third way" in Britain and the "new centre" in Germany, essentially placing yourself between the contending left–right forces and drawing from each to create policies that were sustainable in the long term.

One of the post-Whitlam legacies in Australia is that since 1975 we have been out of step with electoral moods in the northern hemisphere, Fraser having to work with Carter, Hawke with Reagan and Bush senior, and Howard, until Bush junior arrived, with Clinton. The Bush and Howard governments, however, were joined even before September 11 in a backlash against the combination of economic uncertainty and security fears that came with the end of the Cold War. They represent a traditional approach to statecraft and the projection of power that has been losing authenticity for half a century.

In broad outline, the international system we live under came into existence with the treaties of Westphalia in 1648, ending the Thirty Years War and marking the beginning of the end of the Holy Roman Empire and the arrival of the nation-state. The most common way of seeking order in this system has been to check power with power. The Congress of Vienna (1815), using a formula based on British balance-of-power strategic thinking and shared conservative values, was the most successful example, avoiding general war on the European continent until the twentieth century. Sated with wars and revolutions, the twentieth century is often seen as a reaction against nineteenth-century orderliness, but the search for order continued. There were three attempts during the century to form what now was called, to distinguish it from the politics of balance, a New World Order, not surprisingly at the end of periods of war. What was different from earlier attempts to create order was that in the twentieth century they were associated with a single, international organisation not present before. This was the League of Nations and its successor the United Nations. Also, the leading protagonist was the United States, which from its inception had sought a different kind of world order from that envisaged by the Europeans.

If Woodrow Wilson had got his way, New World Order (Mk1) would have been a reversal of the values that had sustained the Westphalian system. The slaughter in the trenches of the First World War brought a reaction against the secrecy and elitism of the system that had fostered the war and the failure of diplomacy to prevent it. Wilson wanted a world order based on principle, not power, in which states would turn from the aggressive pursuit of their individual interests and enter into free association with each other, collectively guaranteeing the security of each, and obeying international law. The first eight of his Fourteen Points spelled out the framework and some crucial specifics: open diplomacy, freedom of the seas, general disarmament, free trade, self-determination for colonies, the restoration of Belgium, the evacuation of Russia and, *sine qua non*, the establishment of the League of Nations.

Wilson's idealism was genuine, although he also believed that what he was proposing was consistent with the interests of a democratic, expansionist and modern America, while it may not have been so comforting for the Europeans. The irony was that his own country weakened the League fatally, while Europe had itself to bear the brunt of the League's failure when fascism turned it into the arena of another world war. Yet Wilson was right in his diagnosis. The system of sovereign states and the idea of balance-of-power as a way of keeping the states at peace without infringing on their sovereignty was proving unstable in a globalising world of new technology and new ideas.

Henry Kissinger, who was born in Europe and saturated himself as a young man in the realism of European statecraft, later becoming Secretary of State in his adopted country, writes in his book *Diplomacy* of Woodrow Wilson's view of the world:

> [His] idea of world power derived from Americans' faith in the essentially peaceful nature of man and an underlying harmony of the world. It followed that democratic nations were, by definition, peaceful: people granted self-determination would no longer have reason to go to war or to oppress others … European leaders had no categories of thought to encompass such views. Neither their domestic institutions nor their international order had been based on political theories postulating man's essential goodness … European diplomacy was predicated not on the peace-loving nature of states but on their propensity for war, which needed to be either discouraged or balanced … The assumption behind all European settlements had been that borders should be adjusted to promote the balance of power, the requirements of which took precedence over the preferences of the affected populations … [6]

As Kissinger acknowledges, without sharing it, Wilson's idealism remains a potent force in the thinking of Americans about their foreign policy. It has been battered by events in the world outside the United States, which do not reveal any underlying harmony, and even by events inside the United States, which often throw doubt on assumptions of humankind's peace-loving nature. It was sustained throughout the Cold War, however, by the American belief in freedom, defined politically as free and fair elections that can change governments, and economically as a form of private ownership that encourages competition and therefore efficiency in producing wealth for everyone.

New World Order (Mk2), expressed after the Second World War in the United Nations, was intended to correct some of the weaknesses of the League. The UN was given the authority and even, according to some interpretations, the military power to deal with breaches of international security (under Article 47, giving the Security Council power to establish a military staff committee, which it has never done). Also important was its intellectual and political underpinning. It was in part a compact between capital and labour, in pursuit of a more just and equitable world. A string of UN agencies was established, such as the International Labour Organisation (ILO) and the World Health Organisation (WHO) in Geneva, the Food and Agriculture Organisation (FAO) in Rome and the United Nations Education, Scientific and Cultural Organisation (UNESCO) in Paris, as well as other specialist agencies and the World Bank and International Monetary Fund. The headquarters of the

United Nations was established in New York, as a way this time of ensuring American public support.

The compact was broken by the Cold War. The international labour movement split into rival organisations. The preamble to UNESCO, which stated that wars began "in the minds of men", was contested by Marxist intellectuals, who maintained that wars were a result of class struggle. The idea that the United Nations would operate as the manager of international security was undermined by Cold War politics, such as the rivalry between the two Chinas for UN membership, the Korean War and, increasingly, the contest between the two nuclear superpowers, the United States and the Soviet Union.

New World Order (Mk3) emerged tentatively when the Cold War ended, in the enthusiasm of the Gulf War in the early months of 1991. The international response to Iraq's invasion of neighbouring Kuwait was so strong and coherent that a common view arose, promoted especially by the American president, George Bush senior, that a new way of securing peace had arrived. The central idea was that the major powers, led by those who had won the Cold War and supported by those who had lost it, would act to contain and resolve conflict, backed by the institutional processes and moral authority of the UN. The rhetoric used by Bush at the time had Wilsonian echoes, and the large vote (144) in the General Assembly to condemn Iraq was an indicator of wide support for a post-Cold War form of security, shown also by the 38 countries which took part in the 1991 Gulf War and the many, especially Japan and Germany, who effectively paid for the expedition. The Security Council was not hobbled by the use of the veto as it had been during the Cold War. In the United States, a feeling also emerged that at last the "Vietnam syndrome" had been overcome – in other words, that the American people had overcome their reluctance to commit American forces abroad after the defeat in Vietnam. But New World Order (Mk3) was short-lived.

The invasion of one state by the armed forces of another was a clear-cut case of aggression which all members of the United Nations could genuinely oppose and, after the shock to the industrial world of the quadrupling of oil prices in the 1970s, a disruption of oil supplies was again feared. Such a compelling combination did not recur. Since then, the challenges to the UN as international law enforcer and peace-keeper have been more complex and UN action less competent and politically attractive. The United States developed a tense relationship with the UN, and the other veto-wielding permanent members of the UN Security Council became restless. The expansion of NATO membership and its intervention in Kosovo, without the imprimatur of the UN, pushed New World Order (Mk3) to the margins of international security.

Now, dealing with the fact of American power, we need to ask whether the two traditional systems of order – balance-of-power and hegemony – or a third, emerging version associated with the League of Nations and the United Nations – voluntary restraint of state power in support of an international regime – offer any guidance in the contemporary world to the need to bring US supremacy into a manageable relationship with other states.

⋆

Off-shore balancing, as it is sometimes called in American commentary, has some American advocates, including Kissinger. It takes a global perspective, looking at the US, European Union, Russia, China, Japan and India as the main players, arguing that the US should now do on a global scale what Britain did for a couple of centuries on the continent of Europe, aligning itself always with the weaker state or combination of states to prevent a single, strong state becoming dominant.

The new global arena exposes some weaknesses of balance-of-power thinking. It works best with a shared value system; today's world is diverse. It requires a continuous shifting of the weight of power to keep the balance – as the British diplomat Sir Eyre Crowe said, in a famous Memorandum, throwing Britain's weight "now in this scale and now in that, but ever on the side opposed to the political dictatorship of the strongest single State ..."[7] While the balance holds, peace is maintained, but when the balance breaks, war follows. Balancing can work in a defined region, where power can be identified and quantified, and where any small change in its disposition is immediately detectable, as was the case in Europe until the First World War, but is it workable on a global basis with more room to manoeuvre and many players in the game, or in a region like Asia-Pacific, where power is so disparate and dispersed that its stability is like a mobile, with states moving around and across each other at different levels?

Even in its heyday, balance-of-power was never quite as clear cut as its proponents believed. By any measurement the Triple Alliance between Germany, Austria-Hungary and Italy in 1882 was a powerful combination, for which Britain according to balance-of-power theory should have sought to create a counterpoise, probably with France, but it did not. The reason was that the British government at that time had more points of friction in its extended empire with France in Africa and with Russia in the Far East than it had with members of the Triple Alliance in Europe or anywhere else, so it argued that the Triple Alliance was good for stability and peace in Europe and allowed it to prosper. Also, external stability did not prevent internal unrest, shown in the outbreak of revolutions in France, Germany, Austria, Hungary and Italy in 1848 and the publication in that year of the Communist Manifesto of Karl Marx and Friedrich Engels. While there was no general war, Prussia extended its borders considerably, first by war with Denmark, then with Austria. A dispute between France and Russia led to the Crimean War (1853–56). Following Prussia's defeat of the French armies in 1870–71, the Paris Commune was formed and, while it lasted only three months, it was a symptom of tension beneath the surface of peaceful Europe.

It has been possible in the past to point to a status quo, in which some, usually the victors in war, participate, and with which others are dissatisfied. A dissatisfied great power was, by definition, a threat to peace. The contemporary world is notable for the absence of any threat to US supremacy from an established great power or group of powers. Today, in so far as it is possible at a time of transition to discern a status quo, there is no dissatisfied power, although there are dissatisfied states. Conflict is now predominantly within states, or, as in the Middle East and South Asia, within regions. So-called "rogue" states and non-state terrorists are the main dissenters from the status quo.

Germany was a dissatisfied power in the twentieth century, but is now content with its role in Europe. Japan was also a dissatisfied power and perhaps, under the surface of its restricted, non-military role as an economic powerhouse, still is. But while the security treaty with the United States holds, the Japanese are part of the winning side in the Cold War and can look to the future with confidence. India is a dominant regional power and a dissatisfied global power, but the latter only in the sense of wanting to be accepted by the status quo powers, especially the United States, rather than wanting to upset the status quo itself. Russia's status is hard to describe. It is unfulfilled rather than dissatisfied.

It had moments of grandeur under the Czars, and an even greater world role as leader of the communist bloc in the Cold War, but its collapse from that height has been as great as its collapse from the rule of the Czars in the First World War. At the moment it is struggling to survive. When that struggle is over it may look to the historically unresolved issues that were overlooked during the search for a universal communist fraternity – whether to face east or west, for example, if it is not possible to do both. China is the most nominated candidate to upset the status quo. It is big and distinctive, suspicious of the presence in its neighbourhood of anyone else, especially the United States. The issue of Taiwan is a permanent trigger. Yet these are also reasons why, if not provoked, China might not wish to disturb the global status quo. It has enough to be satisfied with, and concerned about, within its own territory and region, and has yet to find acceptance as a global player. Europe, sometimes nominated as a great power of the twenty-first century, is still inchoate. It has the substance of power, but not yet the form. At the moment, it has the shape of a loose kind of liberal economic and social order and, increasingly influential as such, could choose to remain as it is.

In other words, the prospective players are not ready for a global balancing game. It is difficult to predict when, or in what circumstances, Europe will develop unified foreign and defence policies. Russia is preoccupied with regaining political and economic stability after its post-Cold War collapse. China is becoming stronger but its influence is still regional, not global. Japan is global but has one hand, military power, held behind its back. India has taken advantage of globalisation adroitly, but is still obsessed with regional security and domestic politics.

Also, the assessment of whether a power should be countered is not simply made on evidence of whether it is quantifiably dominant, but what its policies are and what its intentions are. A dominant power or group of powers which is passive is one thing; a dominant power which is aggressive and threatens you or general stability is another. We do not have the answer to these kinds of questions, as Britain had to the question whether Germany was becoming dominant on the European continent. If Europe does become a great power, how will it act? If Japan does become a fully fledged military power, either in partnership with or independent of the United States, what kind of external policies will it have? Will China be able to withstand the democratising influences of the West's engagement with it?

In addition, does the United States want to play? Balancing is not a role for themselves that Americans instinctively grasp. It is too technical and unprincipled. It lacks both the crusading quality and the bare-faced self-interest that accounts for the support most Americans give to intervention in the affairs of others. They are uneasy with the realism of its politics, the essence of which is the balance, not the morality of those with whom the balancer is aligned. They sometimes try, as in the Nixon-Kissinger period, but they are uncomfortable when they do. It is not moral. In fact, their presence in the Asia-Pacific region as an ally of Japan is somewhat of a balancing role against China, but they do not like to admit it.

They have not yet had the experience of needing to balance the presence of another powerful state in their own region. They overwhelm their hemisphere, some would say divide and rule it, and no challenger has emerged. Powerful outsiders have been dealt with by exclusion. The idea of "equilibrium" is foreign to the popular view Americans have of the United States as "beacon" or "crusader", either of which, or both, are moral imperatives to reform the world, not to ensure its stability. The task of getting the United States to undertake a global balancing role would require a significant shift in this political culture. So when a president arrives with a full-throttle crusade against evil, the world falls into place for many Americans. They have no wish to emulate "perfidious Albion". If there is any model from the past that seems to appeal to them, it is imperial Rome, even the Holy Roman Empire.

So what about hegemony? Peace is managed in the hegemonic model by domination, so that conflict becomes minimal or marginal because there is no substantial opposition to the hegemon. Examples can be drawn from colonial and imperial experience, including the Roman Empire. The Cold War is seen by those who regard it as a long peace as an example of balance-of-power and by those who see it as a long war as dual hegemony, applying especially to the dominance of the Soviet Union in Eastern Europe, but allowing also a softer version of hegemony for the position of the US in its own hemisphere and Western Europe.

Some Americans argue that a degree of hegemony is already in place. You need to be an American to become head of the World Bank. You have to be an American to become military head of NATO. If you want to take advantage of the US's strong position in global media and buy into its assets in America, you have to be an American, as Australia's Rupert Murdoch discovered. Even in the United Nations, the US has more influence than anyone else. It was the only one of the fifteen members of the Security Council that did not want Boutros Boutros-Ghali to have a second term, but he did not get it. If you want something done, you are wise to get the US on side. You can defy the US, as Libya, North Korea, Cuba, Iran and Iraq have done from time to time, but if you do you are likely to find yourself diplomatically isolated and, through sanctions and other constraints, weakened commercially, indeed in some cases impoverished.

However, hegemony is not a concept that Americans have been brought up to admire. They associate it with tyranny. In a pungent critique of Washington's current belief in American power, Hendrik Hertzberg asked in the *New Yorker*, "Whatever became of the conservative suspicion of untrammelled power? … Where is the conservative belief in limited government, in checks and balances?"[8] Also, it is hard to imagine how real hegemony could apply in a globalising world. If the United States wishes to be the world's policeman, it has more than any other state the capacity to do so, but the cost would be enormous. Victory in the Cold War, when only half the world had to be policed, came at a price. "The economy, stupid!" was the slogan that won Clinton the 1992 election against George Bush senior, who was confident after a successful military exercise in the Gulf War of 1990–91. Clinton got the economy moving again, but by 2003 it was buoyed up by huge tax breaks and subsidies to the corporate sector hit by September 11, so that the budget surplus had disappeared and was now in deficit and the US had become the world's greatest debtor state. The American people made their mark as producers and consumers, not as savers. The taxation regime they would need to accept if the US were to try to police the world is beyond the experience of American politics. The most the Clinton regime was prepared to accept as a description of how in today's world the preponderant power of the US should be acknowledged was that it was "indispensable".

As for the third model, voluntary restraint in favour of international agreement, the record of the United States is pretty negative. On the positive side, it generally supports an international regime on issues of free trade and investment. It has blown hot and cold on the International Court of Justice, applauding when its decisions are favourable (as in 1980 when the court ruled for it during the hostage crisis in Iran) and refusing to comply when, a few years later, it found in favour of Nicaragua against US mining of its harbours and support for the Contra insurgents. On the negative side, it opposed the International Criminal Court (120 votes to 7, with 21 abstentions), the Kyoto protocol on climate change (on one vote suffering a result of 178 to 1), a ban on anti-personnel landmines, a treaty on biodiversity, a verification mechanism for the Biological Weapons Control Treaty. It has refused to ratify the Comprehensive Test Ban Treaty, persists with an anti-ballistic missile system, has been recalcitrant on paying its UN dues (and lost its position briefly on important committees as a result), persists in sanctions against Cuba and those who trade with Cuba. It took more than thirty years to ratify the convention against genocide. It has signed but still not ratified the Convention on the Elimination of All Forms of Discrimination Against Women, and, at the time of writing, is only one of two countries in the world that have not ratified the Convention on the Rights of the Child. The other country is Somalia, which has the excuse that it is still trying to form a government that can establish law and order.

These groping attempts to find international agreement on issues on which there is thought to be common ground between states of all shapes and sizes are the early stirring of a global society of states. Law has been such an important civilising agent within states – above all, within the United States – that it is surprising, and disappointing, that the undisputed leader of the contemporary world is reluctant to put its shoulder to the wheel.

★

Many of the key people who clustered around Bush junior and were the most active apostles of the Iraq venture seem to share both the moralism of the Wilsonian tradition and the nationalism of the Washingtonians, but without the internationalism of Wilson or the prudence of Washington. Moral energy, whether evangelical or plain Can-Do American, is certainly the flavour of George W. Bush's administration, but of the Cold War variety, directed at enemies of freedom and with a judicious eye on the strategic interests of the United States.

How did a group of highly motivated and intelligent people around Bush embark on an enterprise so marked by secrecy, deception and confusion that it became both controversial and incompetent, a deadly combination? What chemistry was at work in a decision-making process that was so deficient in the deliberate and careful preparation that is normally associated with a foreign commitment on this scale? Did not the immediate public response flag a warning to politicians normally attuned to public opinion? Whether in the United

States, Britain or Australia it was a mixture of surprise, anger and anxiety. The protest rallies were the biggest since the Vietnam War, the biggest of which, incidentally, were not at the beginning but when the war had begun to turn bad.

Insiders were puzzled by the internal confusion and the sheer effrontery of the public explanations. Retired United States Marine Corps general Anthony Zinni later spoke out, moved to intervene by "false rationales presented as a justification; a flawed strategy; lack of planning; the unnecessary alienation of our allies; the underestimation of the task; the unnecessary distraction from real threats; and the unbearable strain dumped on our over-stretched military". His conclusion: "In the lead-up to the Iraq war and its later conduct, I saw, at a minimum, true dereliction, negligence and irresponsibility; at worst, lying, incompetence and corruption. If there is a centre that can hold this mess together, I don't know what it is."[9]

Trying to understand what might have been the Bush administration's real reasons for moving on Iraq, rather than the reasons publicly given, one arrives at several possibilities. There was, I imagine, a thought that often lurks in the back of political minds, which is the value of distraction. The Americans were caught flat-footed by the terrorists on September 11, 2001, and a wild assortment of conspiracy theories erupted. The official inquiry afterwards revealed a degree of alarm and confusion that would have predisposed the Bush administration to hit back, exerting its proven military power, providing time to recover and to establish an apparatus of "homeland" security. Both in Australia and the United States, public sentiment is attuned to the strategy of expeditionary defence. It is part of folklore that if you engage your enemies abroad, you do not have to deal with them at home, or you can deal with them more effectively at home.

Another reason has been called in the less reverent media, "doing it for Daddy". It is never wise to underestimate the personal factor in high politics, especially in presidential systems. Saddam Hussein had shown himself to be a danger man in the Middle East by his use of chemical weapons against the Kurds and in war with Iran, but he had been supported by the Americans as a lesser evil than the theocratic regime in Iran. By invading Kuwait he showed himself to be not just a tyrant but a brazen adventurer, yet he had been encouraged at a controversial and fateful meeting with the American ambassador in Baghdad, April Glaspie, to think that Washington would not object and when the war was over, and he was thoroughly beaten, Bush senior pulled back, allowing him to remain in power under certain constraining conditions. Bush senior's reasoning was that occupying Iraq would destroy the coalition of supporting allies, turn the Arab world against the US and make a martyr of Hussein. However, he then lost the election that would have given him a second term and Saddam Hussein survived, playing cat and mouse with the constraints, such as no-fly zones, UN arms inspections and an economic embargo. The people who gathered around Bush the son, and probably George W. Bush himself, were convinced that the civilised restraint Bush the father had shown was not appreciated by the American electorate and that their opportunity now was to finish the job he should have done.

On the bumpy ride of public explanations, "regime change" was on-and-off. It was thought that replacing Saddam Hussein with a democratic government friendly to Washington would improve the US position in the Middle East, especially by giving it a more credible and less embarrassing ally than Saudi Arabia. Iraq's oil supplies were almost as substantial. The view of the new conservatives, the so-called neo-cons, was that a new Iraqi regime sympathetic to the US would give Washington more leverage in the Arab world. It seems also to have been the view of a few that a democratic Iraq sensitive to the US would be more sympathetic to Israel. They noted that Hussein had been supported in his invasion of Iraq by another enemy of Israel and another bugbear of the United States, Yasser Arafat. They were also apparently influenced by Ahmed Chalabi, the Iraqi exile who had become close to some at the top of the Pentagon, and who personally was in favour of establishing diplomatic relations with Israel. For doubters who found it hard to imagine how a truly democratic regime, tapping popular feeling, would be any less anti-Israel than other Arab states, the arguments of statecraft were presented. The Japanese had been turned by enforced democracy and a military alliance with the US into a peaceful people engaged in commerce and the accumulation of wealth, and unwilling to stand in the way of whatever it was that the United States wanted to do. Why not Iraq?

Much is made of the strong pro-Israel sentiment in American politics, something which crosses party lines, as shown in important Clinton appointments. In the case of Iraq it had a bearing on the search for weapons of mass destruction. Israel has weapons of mass destruction, secretly developed, undeclared and unchecked by UN inspectors. As India and Pakistan have demonstrated, the simplest case for possession of nuclear weapons is tit-for-tat, and any Arab state's nuclear ambitions would be justified publicly, if necessary, by pointing to Israel's arsenal, already in existence. Against a background of known US support for Israel on this issue, the case against Iraq had to be given a special urgency, by linking it to the September 11 terrorists and by giving it a short fuse. The detail of deception, ambiguity and verbal dexterity in presenting this case has now been documented in telling detail, including, from an Australian perspective, in the book *Axis of Deceit* by Australian intelligence officer Andrew Wilkie, who resigned over the issue.

These reasons merged in the White House with another that was generic, but at the same time very specific, which was to be different from "Slick Willie", also known as the "Comeback Kid". Antagonism to Clinton, more often the Clintons, was at fever-pitch in Republican circles when he was in office. Driving across the United States during the 1996 presidential election, through California, Colorado, New Mexico, Oklahoma, Texas and Arkansas, one got the impression that the entire audience of what is called in America "talk radio" was ready to lynch him. The hosts (not just Rush Limbaugh) and their highly aroused public shared a belief that the man occupying the White House – and the woman by his side – represented all that was untrustworthy and demeaning – despicable would not be too strong a description – about the Democrats, corrupt power in Washington, and (sometimes) the face, or heart, of the entire, wicked human race. It was as if there was welling up in the United States a crusade to cleanse not only the White House and the United States, but the world, of all traces of the Clinton presence. That he won the election easily made it even harder to bear.

The Bushites who captured the White House in the year 2000 were intent, if not on revenge at least on a sharp correction to the way the United States had conducted itself. They wanted to counter the mockery of Cold War heroes, like Nixon and Reagan, and the spirit of compromise and accommodation, rather than triumphalism, that the United States under Clinton had shown to the world. Australian conservatives around Howard shared modestly in some of these feelings about the Cold War. They had had to endure a decade or more of Labor non-triumphalism, Asian engagement and complex multilateralism. But their reasons for going along with Bush on Iraq would have been different and some of these reasons would have been shared with the Blair Labor government in London. I can think of some rationales they shared and one way in which they were different.

Both would have felt after September 11, 2001 that terrorism was a global challenge and that they, like the US, were threatened. Each would have felt that in working to counter terrorism, their relationship with the US was more important than the relationship with their region. This would have extended from the consideration that they might benefit economically in some way in the Middle East from their association with the United States to an acceptance that the Bush people were determined to act and nothing could be done to stop them, so they might as well be joined. The same thought might have passed through the minds of political leaders in Canada and in Mexico, even perhaps in Chile, as well, of course, as in the capitals of Europe. However, at the core of consideration in London and Canberra would have been an element special to them, which was the value of the intelligence links they had with the United States. Intelligence has become an issue in the Iraqi venture and will be examined in more detail later. But we can safely assume that it played a role at the beginning, either in substance by convincing Blair and Howard that the decision to move on Iraq was valid, or by reminding them of the ties that bind, intimate and emotional, compared with the more tenuous, if useful and practical, ties with their regions.

The difference? Blair would have had an additional reason that Howard could not have shared. The British Prime Minister would have felt that the British knew the Middle East, in particular Iraq, as well as the Americans, if not better. Britain had been given a mandate by the League of Nations after the First World War to supervise the creation of what we now call Iraq from provinces of the Ottoman Empire. In a playback of today, with eerie resonance, they set about trying to create a modern state as they knew it. They imported a monarch, Faisal, from Mecca. They established an unrepresentative government with British advisers whose advice had to be taken. They retained their military bases and gave the concession for oil exploration to the Iraq Petroleum Company, actually a conglomerate of British, French, Dutch and American interests. Iraq was eventually admitted to the League of Nations as an independent state in 1932, but the history of modern Iraq is the history of dissatisfaction with this beginning, with power concentrated in the hands of a few with good London connections. Nationalists and communists vied with each other later as true representatives of modern Iraq. The Foreign Office nevertheless prides itself on its subtle insights into the Arab mind and it would have been put to Blair that he could influence Bush to ensure that broader objectives in the Middle East – and British interests –

were not neglected. Howard would not have hoped for such influence. His particular interest would have been, as always, in bringing Australia into as close a relationship as possible with the Americans to ensure future benefits from the alliance.

In all of this, New World Order (Mk4) seems to have been a long way from anyone's mind.

GOOD FENCES

According to the American political scientist Samuel Huntington, Australia is a "torn country" (as he also describes Russia, Turkey and Mexico) because it has mistakenly tried to define itself by economics as part of Asia, instead of by culture as part of the West. Like many Australians, I was surprised by this description. We knew that historically and culturally Australia was Western, but we recognised also the need to be interested and active in our region, and not just economically, without supposing that in doing so we were becoming "Asian". Huntington argued that to escape from the destiny of being torn forever, a "civilisational shift" must occur. The political and economic elite of the country must vigorously support the shift, the public must at least be willing to accept it, and the host – the Asians in this case – must embrace the convert. The second and third of these conditions are not well established in Australia's case. Even the first weakens under conservative political leadership.

In the year 2000 seventy per cent of Australia's trade was with members of APEC and fifty per cent of our exports went to Asia. Yet our cultural, political and military associations were still primarily with Britain and the United States. About 2000 of our university students annually study abroad, most of them in the United States, Britain and Canada. About 115,000 foreigners study in Australia, the vast bulk of them from Asia. Asians come here to learn about the modern world and to become more proficient in English, especially business English. Australians go to the US, Britain and Canada to learn more about the modern world and because they don't need another language. Are we torn or are we just adjusting?

There is a thread of truth in Huntington's description. Australia has a reputation for being casual and friendly, but we are also at times a tense and anxious country, not sure of our position in the region or, indeed, the world, always looking for reassurance that we are not being left "out" or "behind". When Asia was leading the world as an economic powerhouse, with growth rates and trade expansion that attracted not just Australia but everyone, engagement with our region was easy, perhaps too easy, although even then some Australians were concerned that we were being overtaken by neighbours with cheap labour and other non-Australian values. When economic buoyancy subsided and engagement was not with a region of rising prosperity but with a region of complex political, ethnic and religious conflict, the prospect became less inviting and the challenge more difficult.

The American poet Robert Frost put Australia's dilemma succinctly: "Good fences make good neighbours." Australia is physically and culturally detached from its region, but has made a strenuous effort in recent years to be active in it. Like Britain, in its alternating spasms of engagement with the European continent – and Russia, not knowing whether to turn east or west, Turkey, a Muslim nation on the edge of Christendom, and Mexico, alternatively attracted and repelled by its imposing neighbour – Australia's attitude to its region ebbs and flows, zigs and zags, interposing moments of high confidence and creativity with periods of lethargy and pessimism. At the time of writing, it is avoiding the high ground, hoping to occupy a pragmatic area in the lowlands, in which local and global rather than regional factors are dominant. This is a disappointment to those Australians who had seen in the push into Asia a challenge to Australian nationhood that was just about right – not so difficult or dangerous that Australia would be overwhelmed by the task, but neither so easy that it would make no demands on our cultural identity and political independence. Engagement with Asia, it was argued, was a nation-building exercise, a catalyst that would create at last a mature nation.

The current pragmatism is partly a loss of direction. Japan's economic dominance of Asia, on which Australia had for long focussed, has been subsiding, replaced by a mixture of American confidence, South Korean and Taiwanese success and powerful Chinese growth.

In addition, India began to press for more attention. Although India is usually omitted from both the Asia-Pacific and East Asia regions, it is a reminder to Australia of connections that offer a wider range of options than those that press down from the immediate neighbourhood. As a democracy and cricket-playing member of the Commonwealth, India also offers a more relaxing, less demanding, relationship than some nearer at hand, such as Indonesia.

But the current pause is also the result of an early political decision of the Howard governments to pursue a different foreign policy from its Labor predecessors, moving away from regional and multilateral diplomacy and concentrating on the alliance. It proved a useful strategy in dealing harshly with unwanted flows of asylum seekers and in freeing East Timor from Indonesia, but it is a safe guess that the Howard government never expected that its devotion to the alliance would end up with a military commitment in Iraq. When, after September 11, 2001, Australia threw itself behind the United States in the global war on terror, it was the only country in its region to sign up militarily for the initial invasion of Iraq. Others, like Japan, South Korea, Thailand, the Philippines and Singapore, offered assistance later, but none of our Asian neighbours, and not even our Asia-Pacific cousins, New Zealand and Canada, showed enthusiasm for the Bush administration's strategy of pre-emptive military attack.

*

The explanation of Australia's split personality lies partly in history and partly in geography. Founded as an outpost of the British Empire and, initially, as a gaol for the underclass of British society, Australians needed the British, especially the Royal Navy, to protect them from a hostile neighbourhood, in the sense that it was inhabited by large numbers of dark-skinned people following strange customs and religions and hostile also in the sense that it was controlled here and there by rival European powers, like the French, the Germans and the Dutch. As nationalism developed, there was a desire, intense in feeling but tentative in realisation, to dispose of British attitudes to the world in favour of our own. In politics, a dualism developed, expressed by support for British imperialism, including the monarchy and other emblems of culture like the English accent, on the conservative side, and by the Labor Party for a republic, a more nationalistic foreign policy and the Australian accent. But, beneath the political rhetoric, the problem of defence remained.

In statecraft, self-defence is a primary requirement of the nation-state. How it is achieved, whether by military power or diplomatic skill or by association with others is for each country to determine. Until recently, Australians did not believe, either officially or popularly, that we were capable of our own national defence. The belief that the Australian continent was indefensible was a kind of black hole in our attitude to the rest of the world until as recently as the Defence White

Paper of 1987. Unlike say Sweden or Switzerland, which also have precarious security situations, but also highly developed self-defence arrangements to deal with them, Australia neglected civil and national defence and concentrated on foreign policy as defence. Unlike Israel or South Africa under apartheid, we did not arm ourselves to the teeth with powerful, including nuclear, weapons. The idea that Australia was indefensible from its own resources led us to seek the protection of "great and powerful friends", which developed into a strategic doctrine, expressed as "forward defence".

By sending Australian soldiers around the world to fight alongside British soldiers, defending British and imperial interests, Australia was, in the days of the Empire, defending itself. Australian forces went to the Sudan to save General Gordon, to South Africa to fight the Boers, to the siege of Peking, and in two world wars were sent to the Middle East, Turkey, Western Europe and elsewhere. When Japan entered the Second World War, Singapore fell and Darwin was bombed, Australia was vulnerable and turned to the Americans for help. From this wartime association with the Americans, developed another version of "forward defence", closer to home, during the Cold War. The defeat in Vietnam brought a re-examination of its major premise. Was Australia really indefensible? Could we perhaps defend ourselves, at least in most circumstances? The answer in the White Paper was that, in most circumstances short of a major war, we could.

The way force is used in defence of the nation or of the nation's interests becomes over time an expression of a nation's identity. Australia's distinction is that it created for itself a potent martial history without being capable of the basic requirement of defending its own national territory. The Australian fighting soldier, the digger who fought at Gallipoli and in France in the First World War, became one of the icons of nationalism. It was even thought by some that Australia had become a nation, not at the time of federation in 1901, but in 1915 when its young men (and New Zealanders) stood toe-to-toe with the Turks and slogged it out with bayonets on the slopes of Gallipoli. The spirit of the Australian and New Zealand Army Corps (ANZAC) is revived from time to time, although with less enthusiasm in New Zealand, where the spirit of ANZEC (economic co-operation) is preferred.

As statecraft, "forward defence" was pragmatic and, until Vietnam, successful in its own way. It was in Australia's interest to see that Britain continued to rule the waves. Later, when it was obvious that Britain could not, it was in our interests to see that the United States was dominant and especially that it retained a strong presence in our region. It was also cheap. Australia was able to develop into a politically stable and prosperous nation, without burdening itself with a huge defence bill and without provoking neighbours by developing nuclear weapons.

But, depending on others, it was always susceptible

to pressures and self-doubt, and the need to reach an accommodation with our neighbourhood persisted. Australians had been tagged racist because of the White Australia Policy. We showed, through a non-racist immigration policy and the conscious development of a multicultural community, that the tag no longer stuck. The suspicion persisted, however, that we depended for our security on decisions made by a great power on the other side of the world. The post-Vietnam change in defence outlook lifted Australian foreign policy for a while. If the defence of the continent was assured in most circumstances, it was not necessary for foreign policy to place security at the top of its agenda. Australia could undertake diplomatic initiatives that had other objectives than shoring up the power or prestige of a protector. The period of intense activity in Australian foreign policy in its region in the late 1980s and early 1990s was due to the release of Australia from this security preoccupation, coupled with the end of the Cold War.

★

The Australian strategic outlook is quite different from the American outlook described in the previous chapter. One reason was mentioned then, our origins. But the other is that our strategic positioning is entirely different. We cannot expect to dominate our region as the Americans do. We have to accommodate it. What kind of region is it? Quite accommodating.

Australia is not powerful enough to impose its values on our region, but our own values are not threatened. We need leaders who are dexterous, even ambidextrous, in holding to them, while reaching out to others. This requires a subtlety and sophistication that we are still acquiring. It is a slow process, especially culturally. Culture, more than the hard data of economic and military power, is difficult to change. The question often arises whether we can, while remaining allies of the United States, still develop policies of our own in the Asia-Pacific region. The answer is that we can, but we must be prepared to differ from the United States and then to negotiate our differences with diligence and persistence.

- The report on defence by Paul Dibb that preceded the 1987 Defence White Paper was thought by some, including the Americans, to throw too much emphasis on Australia's physical capacity to deny an aggressor and not enough on our capacity to play a role in south-east Asia. The White Paper accommodated this point by giving Australia a capability to project some military power into our region, while retaining the essentials of self-reliance.
- When Hawke announced the APEC concept in a speech in Seoul in January 1989, he did not include the United States in its proposed membership. The speech was intended as a warning shot across the bows of the Europeans and the Americans on trade

issues, especially agricultural subsidies, and it was also meant as a wake-up call to appreciate the economic potential of the region. It had one of the smartest diplomatic responses in history. By the end of the year, the first formal meeting of APEC took place in Canberra with twenty-six countries attending, including the United States.

- Australia's persistence in a peace plan for Cambodia in the 1980s, initially opposed by both the United States and the ASEAN countries, came to a head in 1989 with a proposal by Australia that the United Nations should become directly involved in the civil administration of Cambodia, neutralising the factional and international politics that were left over from the Vietnam War and providing a UN peace-keeping force strong enough to ensure stability for democratic elections. A gruelling diplomatic marathon followed, in which the great powers, the US, Russia and China, the ASEAN states, Indonesia, Malaysia, Thailand, the Philippines, Brunei and Singapore, and the other states of Indo-China, Vietnam, and Laos, as well as the four Cambodian political parties, had to be brought into sufficient agreement for the plan to be realised.
- The Cairns Group of agricultural exporters has fourteen members spanning five continents, including Indonesia, Malaysia, Thailand and the Philippines in our region. It has taken a leading role in opposing

the subsidies both the United States and the European Union give to agriculture. When, in the wake of terrorism-induced defence costs and closer military ties, Australia raised the prospect of a free trade agreement with the United States, concern was felt that the price of success could be Australia's credibility as instigator and leader of the Cairns Group.

The Asia-Pacific region is an important part of the contemporary world. Depending on how it is defined, it has within it Japan, China and ten south-east Asian states, including Vietnam and Indonesia, as well as (in another definition) the United States, Canada and Australia, and (in another) India and even Russia. So its weight and presence are already considerable and it has potential, both as a producer and consumer and also in military power. However, it is not a coherent region in the way Europe is, or the American hemisphere, Christian and capitalist except for Cuba, is, or as Africa, a continent, is. There is no common civilisation, culture or religion: Hinduism, Buddhism, Islam, Christianity, Shintoism, Confucianism, not to mention Communism, are present. Politically and economically it is wide-ranging. Moreover, it is physically spacious and its components are separated by stretches of sea.

A former Japanese prime minister, Yasuhiro Nakasone, provided a valuable insight. He said the differences between perceptions of security in Europe and Asia were like the differences between traditional

European and Japanese painting. In European painting, human detail was important. In Japanese painting, it was the empty spaces that determined the design. In the Asia-Pacific region, it is the empty spaces, not confronting forces, that determine the design. This is reassuring for Australia. I am not aware, for example, of any threat scenario at present, or indeed for some time, that contemplates the actual invasion of Australia.

Asia is geo-strategically spacious, and, unlike Europe, politically and culturally diverse. It has within it states such as Japan, China and India that individually have both disruptive and constructive potential to affect the world. Relics of the Cold War are more noticeable in Asia than in Europe. Unlike Germany, Korea remains divided. China's emancipated province Taiwan threatens independence, and Tibet's spiritual leadership reigns in exile. China, Vietnam and Laos continue as one-party communist states. There is no equivalent of NATO. Its equivalent, the South-East Asia Treaty Organisation (SEATO), set up in 1954 and comprising Australia, France, New Zealand, Pakistan, the Philippines, Thailand, the United Kingdom and the United States, is defunct and the security arrangements that have replaced it are not directed at a particular adversary.

Regionalism in the Asia-Pacific has developed differently from that in Europe or in the American hemisphere. Its style can be traced back to 1967, when the Association of South-East Asian Nations (ASEAN) was formed as a response to the rival pressures of the Cold War, but it is the forum for Asia-Pacific Economic Cooperation (APEC) created in 1989, the ASEAN Free Trade Area (AFTA) established in 1992, and the ASEAN Regional Forum (ARF), which emerged in 1994 as part of a widening consultative process on security issues, that reflect post-Cold War politics in particular. When it first emerged as an Australian proposal, APEC was part of the trade-bloc politics of that time. As the US was not included, commentaries at the time speculated on the possibility of the world being divided into three economic blocs: Europe (with Africa), the United States (with Canada, Mexico and Latin America) and Asia, which, in deference then to the healthy state of Japan Inc., would be a yen zone. However, APEC evolved into "open regionalism", a seeming contradiction that is actually a practical concept intended to reap the benefits of both regional proximity and global free trade and investment.

Regionalism in Asia is thus modest in both purpose and institutions. It survives as a response to the tendency elsewhere and also because of a reluctance in the region to allow the resident powers, Japan and China especially, to assert themselves. Regionalism in this part of the world is therefore inclusive rather than exclusive. Perhaps, some analysts think, it should not be thought of as a region, but as a fusion of Asian and Western cultures and interests. Its essence is networks, not institutions, and the energy of these networks comes from small and middle-size countries, not great powers. Why not value especially the pragmatic spirit of accommodation and consensus, ensuring compromise in the pursuit not of a system of values but better living conditions?

This kind of system has its own way of managing "regime change". It was not shock troops that freed East Timor but a financial crisis that, in Indonesia, the most severely affected of several regional states, brought an abrupt end to the Suharto regime which had dominated politics for more than three decades. International organisations, especially the International Monetary Fund (IMF), took the initiative in dealing with the effects of the crisis. In the case of East Timor's independence, which came to a head as part of the political transition in Indonesia after Suharto's downfall, ASEAN failed to find a role. It was the United Nations and a coalition of interested parties, led by Australia, which forced the pace. This has led to internal debate, especially within ASEAN. Some believe it is time to drop the veto on intervention in each other's internal affairs, which was a founding principle. Others, resisting the change, argue that the principle has been the single most important reason for ASEAN's survival and success.

The regional architecture of the post-Cold War period has developed into something more than scaffolding, but less than a building. Its inclusive, integrative, interdependent and consultative character has been valuable in bringing states together but not in getting them to act. It was constructed at a time of optimism as the Cold War ended, with a bandwagon effect: no country could afford to be left behind. It is seen by advocates of traditional forms of security and trade and investment as fair-weather arrangements that lack the strength and direction to survive a storm. However, it works. There is no present mood to dismantle the scaffolding, but, equally, there has been a loss of energy in the region. Japan's economy has been sluggish for almost a decade and while some of the south-east Asian economies have recovered, they are not attracting capital with the same enthusiasm as before. Some, especially Indonesia, are not yet back on the road to recovery. Also, the United States is beginning to exert itself on security issues in the region, not within the consultative and co-operative security framework of APEC and ARF but in the more traditional form of its own military capability and alliance system. The "gap" between America's actual capacity to defend itself and an abstract idea Americans share that they must make themselves invulnerable to attacks by anyone from anywhere is always likely to be a campaign issue. Sometimes the "gap" does not really exist, as John F. Kennedy found when, after exploiting it against Richard Nixon, he took office. But, in a sense, there is always likely to be a "gap" of some kind, the ideal of American invulnerability being insatiable. The revival of anti-missile defence has created tensions in Asia, especially with China.

Intended to deal with a limited range of attacks from what Washington calls "rogue states", rather than from all-comers as was the case with President Reagan's Strategic Defence Initiative, known as "Star Wars", it comes at a time of proliferation in the development of ballistic missiles in Asia (and in the Middle East) and raises the prospect of an arms race.

So Australia needs to be active in the region, both to look after its own interests but also to keep "open" regionalism alive and well. An argument has emerged lately for a more restricted form, especially in favour of a more "natural" region, East Asia. This is an amalgam of north-east Asia and south-east Asia, comprising the ASEAN states – Myanmar, Malaysia, Thailand, Indonesia, Singapore, Brunei, the Philippines, Vietnam, Cambodia and Laos – plus China, Japan, and South Korea. This group has strong trade and investment networks. It presents the most attractive face of East Asia, although how North Korea and Mongolia can be excluded is a nice point of argument and Taiwan and Papua New Guinea have identity problems, as always. It is supposedly given coherence by "Asian values", based broadly on Confucianism and stressing the responsibilities rather than the rights of individuals. These values are more appropriate than Western values to the needs of developing countries, it is argued, and were the reason why the region first developed as an economic powerhouse. The debate about values subsided somewhat with the Asian financial crisis in 1997. If Asian values were responsible for economic success, why should they not now be associated with failure, especially if this was because Asian states were lax about transparency and accountability? And they do not adequately account for the undercurrent of Muslim values in Indonesia and Malaysia. But they do have one thing in common – exclusion of the United States.

Close relations with the United States create both assets and liabilities for Australia in the region. The US provides military technology and intelligence of a kind that Australia could not manage alone. In addition, it gives a degree of assurance, short of complete but still reassuring, that in the event of threatened aggression against Australia, the United States would be supportive. As an economy the United States is magnetic. On the issue of human rights, Australians have more in common with Americans than with most of the governments and peoples of the region. On the negative side, a strong relationship with the United States supports the view of those who maintain that the region is distorted by the presence of "outsiders" like the Americans, Canadians, Mexicans, Chileans, Australians and New Zealanders, and should confine itself to the true indigenes, like the ten members of ASEAN plus China, Japan and Korea. In particular, Australia's intelligence connections mark it as a member of an exclusive Western club with loyalties outside the region. The old wartime association of the United States, Britain, Canada, Australia and New Zealand continues. Just as the Europeans are suspicious that Britain's intelligence links with the United States give British companies economic advantages over European companies, Australia's close association with the United States arouses suspicion.

These are difficulties that any competent nation in a predominantly pragmatic region should be able to handle. The problem lies not with the alliance itself but with its management at the Australian end. Ministers, including prime ministers, who are overwhelmed by the power and confidence of the United States do not help. Competent and modest men (women seem less impressionable) who become excited by Washington's morality shadow play do not help. The latest victim, John Howard, was trapped by the media into posing as deputy sheriff to the US in Australia's region and later proposed pre-emptive Australian military action in the region not only against the threat of a terrorist attack, but of a conventional military attack as well. A nuclear attack presumably would be dealt with by the Americans. This was one of those moments in Australian history when the mirror falls from the wall, fracturing the Australian image of commonsense. Domestically, there is a political gain. In the region, there is scorn and anger.

There is political gain in Australia because the people are tired of the strain imposed by "engagement" with Asia. An insidious attraction of the alliance is that it is one way of resolving the identity issues that bedevil

Australian involvement, including the debate about Asia's "natural" region and whether Australia is part of it. If neighbours do not accept Australia as part of their community, it should not surprise them if Australia finds comfort in a region defined by American power. Australians would like to be good neighbours, but they do not intend to reinvent themselves to qualify. Some would probably prefer simply to remain as they are, letting the region and indeed the world adjust to them, but they are fewer in number than they were. Most accept that Australia needs to make an accommodation with its region, but they will not accept "Asian values" to hasten the process. If pushed, they might prefer to make the necessary adjustment as an ally of the United States or as a good international citizen rather than as an active member of a regional community.

Drawing on public sentiment, encouraging it to recommit to Australia's necessary engagement with Asia, remains a political test of leadership in this country. It is not the only task for Australian foreign policy, but it is still somewhere at the top of the list.

LOYALTY TO THE ALLIANCE

In one week in the middle of the year – early June 2004 – almost all the issues that this book is examining were raised in the form of media events. On his way to Washington, John Howard called on the former film star Arnold Schwarzenegger, who had become Governor of California, in order to boost the prospects of an Anglo-Australian company, BHP-Billiton, a contender for an oil and gas concession off the Californian coast. His larger strategy, like his push for the free trade agreement while in Washington, was to demonstrate that having the United States as a close friend had an economic dividend. In Washington, Bush announced after his meeting with Howard that Opposition Leader Mark Latham's plan to withdraw troops from Iraq would be "disastrous", saying that it would "embolden the enemy" and "dispirit those who love freedom". Latham responded with a brief press release in which he maintained Labor's position, saying also that the alliance was "bigger and stronger" than the mistakes made in Iraq and that he looked forward to the day when "a Labor government can work with the United

States to further strengthen the intelligence, strategic and cultural relationships between our two countries". Not, it was noticed, the political and economic relationship. Within a few hours, the director of the Central Intelligence Agency, George Tenet, resigned, reviving the controversy over intelligence and the Iraq war. In Singapore for a meeting of defence ministers, the US Secretary of Defense, Donald Rumsfeld, philosophised about the conduct of war, speculating, on the eve of the anniversary of D-Day (the landing on Normandy to begin the last phase of the Second World War), that if General Eisenhower and others had had to fight a war the way he, Rumsfeld, had to, with everyone watching every move, Eisenhower might not have been so successful. In London for meetings with Blair and later at the D-Day celebrations, Howard made all the links of sacrifice and dedication to duty between the fight against Nazi Germany and the fight against terrorism, saying that men had died at Normandy because for too long, too many in the world had ignored a gathering threat. In interviews, he repeated, again, in relation to Iraq, that whatever differences Australians might have had about the war and whatever the links might or might not have been between Saddam Hussein and al Qaeda, now was not the time to change course because the terrorists had "invested enormous resources" in Iraq and a withdrawal would enable them to claim victory. There is a fine line between paying respect to the war dead and glorifying the event in which they died, and political leaders tread it carefully. It was left to one Australian, Dacre Smyth, who had fought on the beach and was now to receive the French Legion of Honour, to put the case for the human horrors of D-Day: "For God's sake, avoid another war."

And in the midst of all this, former film star and former US president Ronald Reagan died. In the tributes that flowed from the governments in Washington and Canberra, his human qualities – optimism, personal decency, humour – were noted by friend and foe alike, but it was as hero of the Cold War who turned the tide against the Soviet Union and forced the demolition of the Berlin Wall that he was particularly remembered. This partial view of Reagan, who was also the president responsible for the Iran-Contra affair, in which members of his staff broke the law in diverting, with the assistance of members of the intelligence agencies, funds from the sale of arms to Iran to the Contras fighting in Nicaragua, and was the president who, in another view of the dynamics of the Cold War, prolonged rather than ended it, dominated the air waves and the screens for a couple of days.

It was a week in which politics and history tumbled over each other in an emotional spectacle of colour and movement, and it was clear that the alliance would be a central issue in the Australian elections. President Bush's word "disastrous" echoed down the corridors of the State Department, with Secretary of State Powell and Deputy Secretary of State Armitage repeating it.

Richard Armitage went further, asserting that the alliance meant political and economic ties – in addition to Latham's military, intelligence and cultural – and it wasn't a menu from which you could pick and choose. The use of the word "disastrous", as it fell on some Australian ears, especially after it was refined by Armitage, had, of course, another possible meaning, which was that it would be disastrous for Australia. Was this a threat that if we elect the Labor party we will be punished, perhaps by cutting off our ration of intelligence or blocking the free trade agreement? This alarming interpretation aroused, in an editorial in the *Age*, a thoughtful question. Was there anything on which the sovereign Australian nation-state could reasonably disagree with the United States without imperilling the alliance? It took a conciliatory smile or two from Powell on television and some welcome words from the Kerry camp to Latham or anyone else the Australian people might elect as prime minister to quell the tremors. They were revived a few weeks later when Armitage repeated what Downer had been claiming for some time – that Labor was split on the issue of withdrawing troops.

What, of course, prompted President Bush to say that Latham's withdrawal would be disastrous, was that it could be unhelpful politically for him, Bush, if an Australian election were held before the American elections and Labor won. He had every right to an opinion, and Australian commentary that it was interference in our internal affairs may have been precious, but it was hard to acknowledge the aptness of the word "disaster" in relation to the withdrawal of Australia's small military contingent nor to any ripple effect it might have. Latham was playing populist politics in saying the troops would be home by Christmas, but by then the situation in Iraq, after six months of Iraqi interim government, could be entirely different and an Australian contribution of a non-military kind more appropriate.

*

The curious thing about the alliance with the United States is that, in Australia, it is divisive. You would expect that because it has bipartisan political backing, broad support in the Australian community, and is generally regarded as the most important security arrangement we have, it would have a unifying effect. In fact, it does not bring Australians together. Rather it creates tensions among us. This in turn engenders sensitivities in our relations with the United States.

The alliance is divisive because it has been handled in a way that has offended Australian sentiment. From the "great and powerful friend" presentation of Robert Menzies through Harold Holt's "All the way with L.B.J." until the flatteringly inter-personal endorsements of Bush junior and Howard, there has been a conscious strategy on the part of the Coalition parties in Australia to lift the bar of enthusiasm for the alliance to a height that their political opponents cannot jump. It is a simple political calculation that began during the

Cold War as a way of playing on the nerves of Labor, which was then split on the issue of how to deal with communism. It reached its peak in the build-up of the military commitment in Vietnam. For a period, after the failure in Vietnam, the influence of Whitlam, Hawke, Keating, Beazley and Evans brought some balance to our appreciation of the alliance, especially as Malcolm Fraser, who was prime minister between Labor governments, was, while anti-Soviet, not effusive about the Americans.

Whitlam resisted the view, pressed on him afterwards, that Kerr's dismissal of his government was the act of a pliant instrument, if not actually an agent, of American intelligence. An earlier example of regime change in Chile had pricked suspicions, coupled with sensational disclosures a few years later by Christopher Boyce, working in US satellite espionage, that the Central Intelligence Agency had infiltrated Australian unions. It was well known that there was concern within the Nixon presidency in Washington with the more independent foreign policy Australia was adopting. We had been critical of American tactics in Vietnam, especially the heavy bombing of Hanoi. But Whitlam was inclined to treat both Fraser and Kerr as home-grown conspirators, working against him with different motives, one political, the other personal, and took them on in open combat, Australian-style, which he lost. Hawke, who was almost as pro-American as he was pro-Israel, while remaining strikingly Australian, was thought to have ended the temptation to play politics with the American alliance, but with Howard it began again. He happened to be in Washington on September 11, 2001 and was naturally caught up in a poignant, tragic and highly dramatic event. But, as a shrewd and experienced manager of Australian politics, he was on sure ground at home and he played the alliance afterwards for all it was worth.

It can be said that this is just politics and it is up to the Coalition's opponents, especially the Labor Party, to see that they don't fall into the trap of being off-side. This is easier said than done when emotions are raised over the commitment of military forces abroad. Lives are at stake and the responsibility for putting people in what is delicately called harm's way is high. The complex issues which the White House has to juggle, including public opinion and relations with Congress, apart altogether from the merits of any military campaign itself, are simplified by the time they cross the Pacific to whether or not Australians are for or against America, or for or against America's declared adversaries or enemies, or for or against democracy or Western civilisation. Or personally for or against the American president. The present prime minister is adept in the use of this tactic. Other ministers, not always so adept, are attracted to high indignation, responding at one stage to any critical questioning with countercharges of "appeasement" and "talking like Saddam Hussein".

In Iraq, as in Vietnam, camaraderie on the battlefield has proved not to be enough. The excitement of Australian combat troops engaged in an important commitment overseas has ground down to an unheroic exercise trying to contain local insurgencies; foreign troops are regarded less as friends and liberators and more as conquerors and oppressors. As the political debate in Australia reached a high pitch in mid-year 2004, Australia had 850 troops in Iraq, compared with 139,000 from the United States. The Australians were engaged in non-combat tasks, such as protecting the embryonic Australian embassy, training Iraqi elements of the army and navy and ferrying humanitarian aid. The Australian government was pained to point out that Australian troops had had nothing to do with the bad things that were happening in Iraq, such as the atrocities at the Abu Ghraib prison or military assaults on the Sunni holdout in Fallujah or on Shiite rebel groups in Najaf and Karbala, while at the same time claiming that they were active in the good things.

Much of the fuss over who is anti-American and who is kowtowing to Washington arises from the elevation of the alliance to a status that is exotically high. It has become the Eleventh Commandment of Australian politics, rather than being respected for what it is, an important instrument of Australian security which is, in turn, one component of our national interest. A valuable asset has become the treasury itself. A useful instrument of the national interest has become identical with the objective it is meant to serve, as if it embodies the national interest, rather than being one of several means of achieving it. In short, there is a confusion of ends and means. The alliance has become an end in itself, as if it requires no other legitimacy than the weight of American authority behind it. And there is also a confusing imbalance between the military and political elements of the alliance. The political alliance is bloated, while the military alliance is starved. In Iraq, as was also the case in Vietnam, the Australian military commitment is too slight to have an effect on the outcome, yet its political value is said to be so great that withdrawal of the troops becomes an issue of national character and principled loyalty, threatening the alliance itself.

Even before the deterioration of conditions in Iraq, keen observers of the Prime Ministerial style, alerted to the way he had used the politics of asylum seekers and border security, had begun to wonder whether he was not pushing his luck. Yes, most Australians value the alliance, but not at any price. Yes, many Australians admire the United States, but it is demeaning for them to be forced to a contest among themselves to decide who can be more loyal to a foreign power. The point was underlined when the Opposition Leader, Mark Latham, cancelled a trip to the United States in June on the grounds that the upcoming election required his presence at home. The Prime Minister contended that the trip had been cancelled because Latham knew he would not be welcome. And the United States ambassador in Australia, J. Thomas Schieffer, made public comments that were interpreted by the Labor Party (and by sober sections of the media) as unnecessarily detailed about Australian domestic politics.

★

The military alliance between Australia and the United States was created in 1951 to deal with a different world from the one we are living in. Forged in the Second World War and formalised afterwards as part of the negotiations of a peace treaty with Japan, and with a future Japan in mind, the ANZUS treaty deals with territories and state instruments, such as "armed forces, public vessels and aircraft", and constitutional processes.

The key provision is Article IV, which states that "each Party recognises that an armed attack in the Pacific area on any of the Parties would be dangerous to its own peace and safety and declares that it would act to meet the common danger in accordance with its constitutional processes." There are two ambiguities. The Pacific area is not defined. In 1958 the Menzies government decided that the Formosa Straits were not in the Pacific area and that it was not an Australian obligation to support any American warship fired upon. Also, while the treaty obliges the parties to "act" to meet an agreed common danger, it does not specify the kind of action they are required to take. Australia was never able to discover in the early 1960s with any certainty whether, if Australian troops were engaged in Borneo in support of Malaysia against Indonesia, the United States would "act" militarily to assist us. The bipartisan support for ANZUS has tended to emphasise its defensive nature. The vehicle for Australian engagement in our region during the Cold War was not ANZUS but SEATO. It was SEATO which was the umbrella for our intervention in Vietnam. It was not ANZUS but a resolution of the United Nations General Assembly that was the authority for our engagement with the Americans in the Korean War (1950–53). Australian forces took part under American military leadership in the Gulf War (1991) not under ANZUS but at the direction of the United Nations Security Council.

New Zealand was originally part of ANZUS. There is no provision for expulsion, but New Zealand became "inoperative" after a row in the 1970s with the United States over the entry of nuclear-armed vessels to New Zealand ports. Australia still co-operates on defence with New Zealand but separately from our co-operation with the United States. By a form of military bracket creep, ANZUS had been edging away in our consciousness from being a defensive arrangement in one part of the world to one that has a global role. It was ANZUS that provided the authority for the joint space-defence facilities that during the Cold War provided the Americans with useful information as the "balance of terror" or of "mutually assured destruction" developed in their nuclear-armed relationship with the Soviet

Union. Perhaps the most valuable aspect of the alliance for Australia is the sharing of intelligence. This arises not from ANZUS itself but from a sharing arrangement with Britain, Canada and the United States that developed during the Second World War and continues, but its chief value to Australia is the intelligence we get from the United States. We get much more than we give.

Australia invoked ANZUS after the terrorist attacks on New York and Washington on September 11, 2001 and there has been a revival since then of wartime rhetoric and camaraderie. "We are in this together" is the familiar rallying cry. Those who were uneasy about the initial martial response were inclined to be patient. The attack was so dramatic and the shock to the American system, political and economic, so sharp, it was understandable that the United States should want to retaliate and that Australia should want it known that we were not just fair-weather friends.

In the United States, the fear and fury over the attacks on September 11, especially the spectacular demolition of the twin towers of the World Trade Center in New York, gave a new president, who had already signalled his intention to be more militant in national defence, no option except to act with the moral energy backed by force that Americans have come to expect. To have turned the other cheek would have invited political oblivion, even impeachment. For the first time, leaving aside the Japanese attack in 1941 on Hawaii, which was in the middle of the Pacific

Ocean, and the British sacking of Washington, including the White House, in 1812 (which was a hangover from the revolutionary war) the homeland, the sacred soil, had been violated. In Australia, there was instinctive understanding of the American response. We had been bombed by the Japanese (in Darwin and the north-west) and one-man, semi-suicide Japanese submarines had popped up in Sydney Harbour, but we had never been invaded and had not even had to cope with the shifting local loyalties of a civil war. Unlike most countries, Australia and the United States have been singularly untouched by the territorial ebbs and flows of war.

In addition, there was something that could be done militarily, and quickly. The Taliban regime in Afghanistan, promoted by the United States during the Cold War to remove the Russians, was known to be providing sanctuary (with the support of elements of Pakistan's military intelligence) for Osama bin Laden and the al Qaeda terrorist organisation, believed to be responsible for the terrorist attacks. So the punitive invasion of Afghanistan, although technically beyond the scope of ANZUS, passed with relatively minor debate in both Australia and the United States. It was a risk, the inhospitable territory having proved a graveyard for interfering foreigners in the past, but it was felt that the Americans had to do something and their cause was just. The Director of the CIA, George Tenet, had said "… we must also look beyond the immediate danger of terrorist attacks to the conditions that allow terrorism to take root around the world … The problems that terrorists exploit – poverty, alienation and ethnic tensions – will grow more acute over the next decade."[10] Afghanistan could be stretched to remain within the range of this analysis.

The extension of the "war" against terrorism to Iraq, however, after an inconclusive and bitter debate in the United Nations, brought to a head a host of misgivings. Sympathy for the United States as the victim of September 11 began to shrink as the President declared a global crusade against evil and leading figures of his administration puffed out their chests and promised a military campaign in Iraq of "shock and awe". The US military build-up was relentless and the rhetoric on the threat of weapons of mass destruction highly charged. The vice-president Dick Cheney is on record that there was "no doubt" that Iraq had weapons of mass destruction and links with al Qaeda. The President's national security adviser, Dr Condoleezza Rice, in a startling presentation against further UN weapons inspections proposed that if we took more time looking for a "smoking gun", we could find ourselves faced with a "mushroom cloud".

Much attention was paid to the immediate effect of US military power, while the longer-term consequences of intervention were not examined. It was assumed that after a contest of force, which the United States would win, there would be a union of liberating troops and joyful Iraqi people. Instead, as Napoleon discovered in Moscow in 1812, and as some powerful armies have learned since, there was no brave, futile resistance, just a melting away, allowing the acrid ruins of bombed cities and the bitter history of ancient feuds to test the triumphant invader.

In Australia, the Howard government was enthusiastic, to an almost feverish degree, about the extension of the war. The language of the Prime Minister, the Minister for Foreign Affairs, Alexander Downer, and the Minister for Defence, Robert Hill, reflected the buoyant mood in Washington, brushing aside the concerns of defence analysts and former military leaders. The pessimists had been wrong about Afghanistan and they would be wrong about Iraq. We were taking the fight to the enemy, who was threatening the civilised world. As more specific reasons were under Washington's control, Canberra was not able to do more than keep in step as they were released. Even that was sometimes difficult. There were so many reasons that it seemed at times the government was protesting too much. There was the threat of weapons of mass destruction, and the need to rid the world of a brutal dictator and the opportunity to establish a more promising prospect in the Middle East and global responsibilities for peace and prosperity. None of the reasons was singly compelling. We knew that Saddam Hussein had used chemical agents against the Iranians and Kurds, that he had deployed biological weapons and that he harboured a desire for nuclear weapons. But the UN inspection team over the years had, despite his resistance, done a good job. There was overwhelming evidence that Saddam Hussein was a brutal dictator, but he was not the only one around and there was no evidence that he was in some way connected with the terrorist attacks on the United States, or was now a threat in the sense of being a "clear and present danger" to the United States or Australia. A democratic regime in Iraq, responsive to the United States, would be in principle an improvement, and it might have been thought by some in Washington that a display of brutal American power in the Middle East might have a salutary effect wider than within Iraq, but in relation to stability and especially the security of beleaguered Israel, the prognosis was dubious. In any case, the divine right to impose regime change around the world was not something the world was ready to grant the United States. As for global peace and prosperity, there was an inclination to see this as a cover for one of America's enduring national interests, access to supplies of oil.

There is no indication in the record so far that any alternative, or even mild corrective, to Washington's approach was suggested by any of the Australian agencies or departments involved, including the Department of Foreign Affairs and Trade. The decision having been made in the White House, we followed suit. At the core of official rhetoric at the Australian end, however, sometimes obscured by the hard bites of "national interest" and lost in the floral perfume of patriotism, was an enduring reason, the importance to Australia of the alliance with the United States. It was the cement that held all the mismatched and contradictory bits of the story together.

What was not expected was incompetence. The Iraqi expedition as it unfolded had the feel of something planned with speed, secrecy and perhaps in great excitement without much thought for what followed. It is hard to imagine how such a major exercise could have been planned and executed without budgetary provision for reconstruction after the military invasion. The 21-day assault in March–April 2003 was highly effective but the intelligence of what to expect was not. Understanding of the religious and cultural make-up of Iraq, especially its mix of Sunnis, Shiites and Kurds, seems to have been slight and there was a failure to appreciate the value of Iraqi business opportunities. The lion's share of the early contracts went to the American corporation Halliburton, creating disappointment in Iraq and political uproar in the United States, as Vice-President Cheney had earlier been chief executive of the giant military contractor.

There were not enough troops on the ground to maintain security. The Iraqi army was disbanded, and then revived. Hand-picked Iraqi leaders who would accept the return of their country's sovereignty from the occupiers on the smart change-over date of 30 June turned out to lack popular following, while those who had a following turned against the Americans. As the situation became increasingly chaotic, the US fell out with Ahmed Chalabi, a prominent Iraqi Shiite exile who had been on the Pentagon payroll for four years and touted as Washington's choice to become leader of the new Iraq. Washington handed over the job of finding a credible group of Iraqi leaders to a United Nations official, Lakhdar Brahimi, a Sunni from Morocco, who had managed the transition in Afghanistan.

★

In the midst of the confusion came the discovery, with graphic pictures shown all around the world, that, for several months beginning late in 2003, American guards had been subjecting Iraqi prisoners to humiliating forms of torture in a gaol, Abu Ghraib, on the outskirts of Baghdad. An outburst of anger and disgust was all the more poignant because Abu Ghraib had been, during the regime of Saddam Hussein, a notorious centre of incarceration, torture and execution. Australian forces were not directly involved, but the revelations were an embarrassment to the Australian government by association, as so much had been made of the superior moral values of the invaders, Australia, Britain and America, who were there to free the Iraqi people from the degrading brutality of Saddam Hussein.

Official responses adopted a high, moral tone. This is not the way we expect our soldiers to behave and we will show how different we are by the way we bring this into the open and punish those who did it. It was a predictable defence, sound because it was accurate. True, it was not government that had disclosed the offensive behaviour. It was outraged insiders, assisted by helping hands in the media, but they were as much a part of a free and open society as government. No such outcry had occurred in Iraq in the glory days. The official response did not, however, stem the flow of blood. For a start, Australian ministers might applaud the democratic virtues when in full flower elsewhere, but when they came to bear on the ministers themselves, applause changed overnight to wounded cries of indignation. A study will no doubt eventually emerge of the Minister for Foreign Affairs (Mr Downer) in full flight in the House of Representatives on the Australian issues arising from Abu Ghraib, his indignation high, his contempt for his critics palpable. His countercharge that the reputation of gallant Australian soldiers serving in Iraq was impugned so overwhelmed his answers to questions about Australia's responsibilities as part of the coalition occupying Iraq that it was not always clear what he was actually saying. So far as could be determined, the situation was that, under the Geneva Conventions, Australian soldiers who captured Iraqis and handed them over for detention were required, or their government was required, to ensure that requirements of the Conventions were met by the "detaining power", in this case the United States. Australian soldiers had evidently captured 120 prisoners and handed them over to the Americans. Australian military personnel had made several visits to Abu Ghraib and had reported back to Canberra, both to the Department of Defence and the Department of Foreign Affairs, concerns about the treatment of prisoners. The opposition now wanted to know whether the ministers had known of the reports and, if so, when, and if not, why not? For ministers whose minds are gripped with great purposes, these are irritating questions, but they have to be asked and answered. The Minister for Defence (Senator Hill) said he knew nothing of the Abu Ghraib abuses until the media disclosures, and the Secretary of the Defence Department (Ric Smith) and the defence forces chief (Peter Cosgrove) accepted responsibility for a "failure of communication". Something had gone wrong, as it had so often in the Iraq venture. The issue dragged on day after day in parliament, leaving an impression that information about prisoner abuse in Iraq had been buried in the bureaucracy for some time and no-one had realised its significance until pictures appeared in the media. This, in itself, was a startling disclosure.

In the United States, the issue had a double prong: not only who knew about the abuse but who was responsible for it. Although the US army had known about the mistreatment of detainees at Abu Ghraib and had asked for a report, it was not clear how far up the chain of command the knowledge had gone. The Secretary of Defense, Donald Rumsfeld, accepted responsibility because it happened on his watch, but declined to resign. Congressional leaders had not been informed and were upset, especially those who had backed the President over Iraq.

And the pictures themselves, as they poured out in a seemingly endless stream, raised questions about the discipline and morality of the United States military forces. They were sadistic and brutal and, in addition, peculiarly sexual, involving naked men, masturbation and intercourse, and were remarkable because the more lascivious of the guards were women. Why had the pictures been taken? They were like trophy snaps, the lion killer with his foot on the neck of the once savage beast. Or, perhaps the heaped naked bodies overseen by a smiling gauleiter with folded arms were meant to be a reminder of the Holocaust, or a masturbating male of Hannah Arendt's "banality of evil". Was the hooded scarecrow figure, with electric wires dangling from his fingers, a reminder of the Ku Klux Klan? It seems not. The pictures were apparently intended as a form of intimidation, drawn from the continuously refined and updated experience of the torture professionals, whose job it is to extract information from unwilling victims. They were intended to be shown to future batches of Iraqis, caught in a sweep of the usual suspects, as a warning of what they might expect if they did not "loosen up" and tell their interrogators what they wanted to know. They were explicitly sexually humiliating because they were meant for Iraqi men whose culture led them to assert their authority over women and to despise homosexuality.

What happened at Abu Ghraib represented in microcosm the confusion that seemed to reign over the entire American presence in Iraq. An army major general, Antonio Taguba, who prepared an internal report, concluded there had been a complex breakdown of leadership, discipline and training, involving the intrusion of military intelligence and private contractors into the chain of army command. He noted that Abu Ghraib was filled beyond capacity and that more than 60 per cent of its inmates were wrongly detained, in the sense that they were not a threat to the military occupation, or to Iraqi society.

The Abu Ghraib incident, and later revelations of other abuses by American soldiers at other gaols in Iraq, raised fresh issues in the debate about Iraq. The Geneva conventions, US army regulations, American public mores, the pressure from the Bush team to get results from the interrogation of prisoners and the Nuremberg precedent that obeying orders was no excuse were all under scrutiny. A series of leaked legal memoranda in Washington revealed that, since late 2001, in preparation for a dirty war on the terrorists, US policy makers at a high political and military level had been examining ("musing" said the White House) how to evade international rules and conventions on torture.

★

As the situation in Iraq deteriorated, official Australian rhetoric became more careful and precise. We were there because we were not the kind of people to cut and run. We were there, small in number but high in quality. There was still a job to do, like training elements of the Iraqi forces and guarding the Australian mission. But any mention of the alliance again quickly raised the temperature. The Prime Minister, in a carefully prepared speech on 19 May in defence of the decision to send Australian forces to Iraq, expressed the opinion that the US was the only nation able to change the world for the better and that the commitment to Iraq had become "ultimately a test of character and leadership – whether we possess the necessary determination and resolve to meet our commitments to the Iraqi people or whether we will retreat in a pointless attempt at isolationism". At about the same time, at the signing of the free trade agreement with the United States in Washington, Australia's Minister for Trade said, "This is the commercial equivalent of the ANZUS Treaty ... The blood of young Australians and Americans has been shed on most continents of the world in defence of our shared ideals of freedom and democracy."[11] His US counterpart, Robert Zoellick, praised the alliance as "that special belief in humankind" that draws America and Australia together "arm in arm" from Afghanistan to Iraq because "we will never accept tyranny as the natural order".[12]

For insiders, this was code language, meaning this is

reward for being such a staunch ally when we are in such a pickle. But in the public arena, it had a desperate ring. It could not disguise the fact that the alliance had drawn Australia into a situation that was embarrassing at the least but also fraught with serious consequences and responsibilities over which we had little if any control. And it could not disguise another fact, which is that the free trade agreement needed to pass scrutiny in the Senate not on whether it was a payment for blood on battlefields but whether it was of economic value to Australia.

The return of the United Nations in June 2004 to the scene of the crime went some way to stabilise a situation that was getting out of hand. Kofi Annan's steadfast interest and the useful diplomacy of UN official Lakhdar Brahimi helped produce a broad-based, interim government to represent the sovereign Iraqi state that came into being at the end of the month. A unanimous Security Council resolution established the terms of the relationship between this government and the foreign military forces already in Iraq, leading up to elections early in 2005 and a new constitution. From the UN itself came careful and sensible comments on the intention of the resolution (based on the Security Council's right to enforce a peace, not just to keep it), its limitations and the fragility of both politics and security in Iraq. It was a relief to have moderate language on the airwaves and modest faces on the television screens.

The situation in Iraq now precisely mirrors the ambivalent attitude towards the United States in this book that readers will have already detected. A tyrant has been removed and the first, hesitant steps toward democracy have been taken. Good. The use of force by the Americans to impose their will on a country that was unfriendly but posed no threat to them has been confirmed. Bad. Democracy, yes! Imperialism, no! The argument goes on.

There is still a long way to go before stable government in whatever form it evolves is established in Iraq, but UN intervention has given legitimacy to regime change at a time when most of the Iraqi people (opinion polls said 80 per cent) and the rest of the world had grave doubts about both the legitimacy and the authority of the United States. Both Bush and Howard took the view that the UN was now giving legitimacy to what they had done a year before, but a more widely held view was that the UN had rescued them from a foolhardy and mismanaged venture that was courting disaster. In the United States, the Bush administration had to face some moments of truth, and there were signs that it was bending to the wind. The President began to refer to a "multi-national" force rather than a "coalition of the willing". He formally accepted Tenet's resignation as director of the CIA, who had advised him that the discovery of Saddam Hussein's weapons of mass destruction would be easy (a "slam-dunk" in one version). Tenet's departure, from Bush's standpoint, would establish the principle that the advice the President had acted on was faulty. The new ambassador, Philip Negroponte, who had been ambassador to the UN, spoke in measured tones about his job, its relationship to the interim Iraqi government and to the command of the American forces in Iraq. The John Kerry camp, while keeping its distance, seized on the political shift to sovereignty and the supportive mood in the UN security council to indicate that it would stay the distance to back Iraq's transformation to democracy.

In Australia, however, the election roadshow continued. Howard, in a major foreign policy speech to the Australian Strategic Policy Institute, ground relentlessly on about Mark Latham's anti-Americanism and his own acceptability in Washington. He spoke about the great and noble purposes of US foreign policy and in a strangely un-Australian phrase of Labor's narrow view of the alliance that "would circle the wagons" and deny Australia the capability to co-operate with allies beyond our shores. It was a speech in which the entire bundle of trouble, rogue states, failed states, weapons of mass destruction and terrorism, was presented as a challenge to Australia that needed to be met with the full thrust and power of the alliance with the United States. As a political speech, it might or might not (I have no way of telling) have been cleverly targeted, but as a statement of Australian foreign policy it was insensitive and negative, insensitive because it ignored all the evidence of Australian concern about being too close to

Washington, and negative because it passed up the chance to reach out for a bipartisan approach to the new sovereign Iraq with a timetable for elections. In July, Hill and Downer were in Washington to sign agreements with the US for military training facilities in northern Australia and for an Australian role in the US missile defence system. The timing ensured that the alliance was kept high on the agenda of election issues.

OPTIONAL AUSTRALIA

A combination of American hubris and Australian loyalty has exposed a weakness in our alliance. The Americans under George W. Bush are too entranced with their exceptional virtues and global military reach to pay attention to the voice of a marginal player, and we under John Howard are too concerned with our need for American protection to raise our voice. We each protest that we do otherwise. Washington says it values our opinion and listens to us and Canberra says we make our own judgments in our own national interest, but the facts suggest that neither of these occur, at least in a crisis. It is an old issue, embedded in the power gap between the two countries; it has come to a head again because of the intervention in Iraq and because the occupants of high political office in each country, Bush and Howard, share a world-view. The result has been a deep division of opinion in both countries, weakening the alliance.

The divisive effect in Australia exists at two different levels. On one level, there is a straightforward, publicly documented division of opinion about the prudence and efficacy of the intervention in Iraq as a response to the terrorist attacks on the United States on September 11, 2001. Public opinion was against the war at the beginning, and has waxed and waned, depending on the course of the military conflict, casualties, media revelations and the ebb and flow of the political debate. Insider opinion has also been divided and, as best one can judge, is more negative than positive. The use of military power can sometimes be effective, quelling disquiet, wrong-footing dissent, at least in the short term, but in this case the whole exercise has been confused, controversial and at times incompetent. Whatever the motive was for intervening in Iraq, its effect on terrorism has been to make matters worse. Even the most brutal justification, which is that it's only worse for the Iraqis, not for Australians and Americans, has yet to be confirmed. The virulent anti-Americanism of the al Qaeda brand has spread as the America of George W. Bush has revealed itself in words and action, more often than not clumsy and insensitive. The International Institute for Strategic Studies reported earlier this year that al Qaeda membership had increased since the invasion of Iraq and now numbered some 18,000 in 60 countries. A hornet's nest of fresh anti-Americanism has been stirred up, while little, if anything, has been done to deal with the anti-Americanism that was already there.

Supporters of the intervention have had little joy, while opponents have had an embarrassment of errors.

As election doomsdays approached, the assenting camaraderie became more desperate. The American President and his highest officials were entangled in Australian politics in a manner never experienced before, even when Whitlam and Nixon collided over the bombing of Hanoi. The Howard government trapped itself in a position of such high attachment to the alliance that not only its political opponents at home but otherwise friendly governments abroad found it oppressive. The Foreign Minister's criticism of Spain and the Philippines for encouraging the terrorists by withdrawing troops from Iraq makes the point. Spain's act was an election promise, made before the terrorist attack in Madrid on March 11, 2004 in which 191 died. Manila's decision was certainly in response to a threat to execute a hostage, but it was made because of the exceptional circumstances of the Philippines as an exporter of domestic labour. It has unprotected potential hostages all over the Middle East.

In the lead-up to the Australian elections, a letter signed by 43 former Australian military chiefs and senior diplomats declared: "We are concerned that Australia was committed to join the invasion of Iraq on the basis of false assumptions and the deception of the Australian people." The letter called for a return to "truth in government". In an explanation, one of the signatories, Ron Walker, said he and others would not have accused the government of deception "if we only believed it had been misled by faulty intelligence".

The letter argued that the war had been destructive, especially for Iraq, had put the international system under stress, and had given Australia a higher profile as a terrorist target. Among the signatories were former chiefs of the defence forces, heads of the navy, army and air force, heads of the departments of Defence and Foreign Affairs and Trade and of the intelligence agencies, including the Office of National Assessments. This was unprecedented. No such massive defection of insider opinion had occurred during the Vietnam War.

A stronger and more confident prime minister might have engaged these elders of the military-diplomatic community in a discourse, on the "national interest" perhaps, but this prime minister is fighting for his political life, not only against his political opponents but also against those in his own party who share the widening perception that the Iraq mission was mistaken. His response was to attack. They were wrong and if the letter said that he had "lied" it was itself a "lie". He pointed out that all except one of the signatories had retired before September 11, 2001, implying that they were ignorant of the new age of terrorism, and one of them was on record with an unjustified attack on the navy. He declined to correct a party member who had described the signatories as "doddering daiquiri diplomats" and another who had described them as "disgruntled old men". And when Latham at question time noted the distinguished war record of several, he attacked the questioner as the last person in parliament entitled to raise ethical issues.

Even the free trade agreement with the United States, comprehensive, technical and of long-term significance, became a political battlefield, to be decided, like Iraq, under the pressure of a contrived timetable and bluster about loyalty to the alliance. It was hustled in the same way that the invasion of Iraq was hustled: it was in the national interest because it was a vital part of our relationship with the United States and if you were against it you were anti-American. This debauched the national interest in the guise of promoting it. There were several problems with the agreement, apart from the government's curiously naive argument that because the United States had ratified it, we should not look a gift horse in the mouth.

There were sharp disagreements among the experts about the benefits for Australia. The government's figure of $6 billion net gain annually was widely disputed. There would be a cost to our major Asian trading partners. There were concerns that the effect on Australian culture and the pharmaceutical benefits scheme would be erosive. In the manufacturing sector there were worries about jobs. Moreover, it was not consistent with the spirit of "open regionalism" promoted by Australia in the Asia-Pacific region, as part of the laborious multilateral "rounds" on freeing up trade that eventually turned the General Agreement on Tariffs and Trade into the World Trade Organisation. "Free trade agreements" are preferential arrangements that create freer trade between the signatories, but not with anyone else. The complex detail made it difficult for the public in the atmosphere of an election to form any more than an impression of whether it was, on balance, in Australia's interest. In any case, the Howard government was untrustworthy. Its record on asylum seekers and Iraq, not to mention the American alliance, made obligatory a review with some degree of detachment, which was what was intended with the Senate inquiry which the government opposed but which eventually allowed the free trade agreement through with crucial Labor amendments.

Generally, the government struggled in the contest for public approval at this level. It fared better at the other level on which public opinion is divided, whether military power is the best way of dealing with the kind of human turbulence that is emerging in the contemporary world and of which terrorism is a part. Here, the debate is rarely explicit, often in code, yet there are clearly two different world-views. One is that the world is divided into zones of peace and zones of turmoil. The prosperous, stable and democratic Western world, including Australia and the United States, occupies the zones of peace, with some others, like Japan, who want to be part of the West, while most of Africa, the Middle East, south-eastern Europe, the territory of the former Soviet Union and a good deal of Asia and Latin America are in zones of turmoil.

This is a version of the Cold War concept of developed and developing countries, but its organising principle is different. The objective is not to capture the hearts and minds of people in the developing world, but to keep them in order. If you see the world this way, the use of military force by those in the zone of peace to deal with imperfection in the zone of turmoil is necessary and justified. The alternative is to leave them to stew in a malodorous mix of tyranny, poverty and massive abuse of human rights, which can become dangerous for everyone.

The use of force is also itself a source of satisfaction. It is thought necessary by some to defend territory and values and its use makes them feel safer. More than that, its speed and finality are impressive, it provides emotional release, even in tragedy, and it is an appropriate form of punishment for those who live by the sword and should now die by the sword. Diplomacy, by contrast, is time-consuming and riddled with compromise. Law, while majestic in its impartiality, is unrealistic when applied to external events, where neither people nor states are law-abiding and its judgment is shadowed by national passions and uncertain outcomes. Most weight in this world-view is on the side of the Bush and Howard governments.

The other world-view is that the world is not divided into two zones, but into three tiers. On the bottom are six billion or so people, most of them poor, many of them in need of food, clothing and shelter, or, if better off, seeking assurance that their lives, their property and the social tissues that bind them in communities are not threatened. In the middle are two hundred or so nation-states, who divide up the world's people and the world's territory among themselves. They are diverse in every respect, culture, religion, economy, politics, but most of them are in regional organisations, which blend their strengths and weaknesses, and almost all are members of the United Nations. On the top, the third layer, are a dozen or more global institutions and organisations, including the UN and its agencies, which are attempting to put together rules and strategies for international security, global governance and civil society. Generally speaking, the world's six billion or so people only have a voice at the third level through their governments, although non-government organisations (and the media) are active at all levels.

A feature of the contemporary world, according to this world-view, has been the rapid development of international law to deal not just with arguments between states about their sovereign rights on the second level but with abuse of the human rights of the world's billions of ordinary people, often by the states themselves. Slowly, the rights of people as human beings and not their duties as citizens of the state are gaining ground, both in the decisions of national jurisdictions and in international tribunals. A kind of double helix of sovereignty is emerging that we have not seen before – that of the state, which we know well in international politics, but also that of the individual, which we have only encountered before within states. The Secretary-General of the United Nations, Kofi Annan, set the scene when he announced to the UN General Assembly in September, 1999 that the world had now to deal formally with two forms of sovereignty. State sovereignty needed to be redefined, he said. States were now widely understood to be instruments at the service of their people, not vice versa. Individual sovereignty, by which he meant the fundamental freedom of each person, was at the core of the UN charter and subsequent international treaties. The world – and therefore the UN – could not stand aside, he said, when gross and systematic violations of human rights were taking place, and the task now was to see that intervention was based on legitimate and universal principles.

But the international regime does not have the means to intervene militarily in the affairs of states. It has no armed forces, no powerful weapons, no intelligence technology except what it can borrow from its member states at a time of need. So the states are being asked to operate as a kind of connecting road between the people and a system many of them do not like and few understand. It is a crucial, confusing development in world politics, thwarting the state's authority, sometimes impugning its integrity, questioning terms like "national interest", "vital interest" and "sovereignty". It calls for a new kind of political leadership, providing national resources for internationally agreed purposes.

It calls for national leaders who are lateral thinkers and ambidextrous rather than leaders who are stalwart and single-minded, and the contemporary world is an increasingly dangerous place for ordinary people because there is a conspicuous lack of this kind of political leadership. A three-layered world, in which the state is broker between the rights and duties of its citizens and an emerging international regime, is not the way history and geography have prepared us to appreciate political leadership. Yet it is increasingly the nature of the contemporary world.

Clinton in office showed glimpses of what is needed, and in his book *My Life* he reflects on this kind of leadership. He points to the economic interdependence of states as a consequence of globalisation and argues that, in respect of security, the process needs to go further, to what he calls "integration". In effect, he is warning his fellow Americans against hubris; they should use their current pre-eminence to integrate peacefully with the rest of the world, so that when their supremacy fades, as it will, they also will be safe. For Australians, this kind of thinking needs to be noted carefully. A peaceful future for us depends on our ability to live in the same kind of world as our neighbours. The lesson of Iraq is not that, as a reaction against a mistaken intervention, we might become "isolationist", prevented from co-operating with our great and powerful ally. The lesson of Iraq is that we need more allies of the integrated variety, with whom we can work to manage the turbulence.

Both sides agree that intervention is at times necessary. It was necessary in the former Yugoslavia, in Rwanda and East Timor, in Somalia and Sierra Leone, in Afghanistan. It is currently necessary in Sudan. The question is: who decides what form the intervention takes? There is the Iraq model, which is at odds with the traditional "blue helmets" form of UN peace-keeping but also at odds with more recent models like East Timor. In the last, the energy and resources of some interested states, enabling them to act quickly as "coalitions of the willing", are available for action, sometimes on their own initiative, sometimes prodded into action by the UN, but requiring the approval of the UN Security Council when the government of the state to be entered does not agree. It never works without travail, but it does work. Consider the difference it would have made in Iraq if the invaders had had the legitimacy of a tick from the Security Council, and a more substantial array of allies. That the United States did not get approval was not the fault of the international system but of the White House's own remorselessly flawed determination to go in on its own terms.

Elections in Australia and the United States, as well as (postponed and almost forgotten) in Afghanistan and later in Iraq, will, in a rough and ready fashion, deliver judgment. In the United States, the test of the election is one of leadership, Bush's leadership of America and America's leadership in the world. Bush is by temperament insouciant, like Reagan, but Reagan appeared on the scene to jolly up Americans after Vietnam, Watergate and other presidential indignities, not in the middle of them. The credibility of government under Bush, the list of dubious, deceitful and incompetent decisions, is a lot of baggage to take into an election.

The alternative president, John Kerry, is calibrating carefully his opposition to Bush. As a senator, he voted for the Iraq mission. Then, a year later, competing against anti-war Howard Dean in the run-up to the 2004 Democratic primaries, he voted against provision of funds to continue the mission. Hence, in the eyes of the Bush campaigners he is Mr Flip-Flop. Kerry, however, is a decorated Vietnam War hero who later turned against the war, while Bush avoided service in circumstances that are unclear. Also, Kerry can claim, supported by the stream of inquiries about intelligence failure and political spin, to have been initially misled by his president. His political advantage lies in exploiting domestic issues left unattended by the focus on war and in restoring integrity to the White House, but he cannot forget that as commander-in-chief he is expected by voters concerned about their security in a threatening world to be "strong". He is more internationalist than Bush and less of a crusader, and he would obviously provide an opportunity for a shift of direction in American global leadership, repairing the damage to former allies, like the Europeans and Japan, but he is less innovative than Clinton and less idealistic than Jimmy Carter.

Of the four political leaders and potential leaders of the United States and Australia, John Howard and George Bush are set in the mould of the traditional nation-state. Howard is adept at capturing patriotic indignation, in the tradition of Billy McMahon raising his fist against the recognition of Communist China or Billy Hughes doing the same against the Japanese at Versailles. His style, politically shrewd and emotionally flat, leads one to assume that he knows what he is doing. His "deputy sheriff" and "pre-emptive strike" remarks are part of the man. That's the way he is. It is shrewd because bits and pieces of the Australian electorate – the Australian battler, working families, diehard patriots, the remnants of Pauline Hanson country and probably many ordinary voters – are closer to him on this issue than to those with a more complete view of the contemporary world. The third tier seems a long way away from people in the bottom tier.

Australia's role in Iraq, at the beginning, throughout and now, has been as follower, not as leader, almost it has seemed at times from Washington's viewpoint, an optional military extra, although politically, for someone lacking substantial allies, valuable.

Howard's problems are thus different from his friend's in the White House, but he, too, has been weakened by both the incompetence and the controversy of the Iraq commitment, the sense that it was mismanaged because of an unhealthy mix of paranoia and arrogance and a feeling, vague yet persistent, that the use of huge military force is not the way to deal with terrorism. Like Bush, he also is presenting himself as a "strong" leader, although neither he nor his lieutenants Alexander Downer and Robert Hill have experienced war or wartime leadership before.

A feature of their leadership has been an aggressively partisan stance, as if their political opponents are in league with the country's enemies or whose own record is so tawdry that they have no right to call the Howard government to account. This has created an offensive, fault-finding style of leadership that does not sit at ease with the call to show patriotic unity and to pursue the national interest. Howard seems not to recognise that as prime minister he must be called to account for what the government does. He seems incapable of reaching out to opponents, either on human or national issues, which our strongest prime ministers knew how to do, or did instinctively. His competent management style presents a jauntily embattled leader when the moment calls for accommodation.

Mark Latham is the least predictable of the four. He has no experience of war or of leadership in war, so his appeal as a "strong" leader is hard for the public to assess. With an experienced Kim Beazley now at his side and Kevin Rudd's established competence in foreign policy, Latham may well not bother to become a student of national defence, as John Curtin did and as Gough Whitlam, Latham's mentor, never did. Latham's interests are primarily domestic, especially the role of social capital and civil society, but he is one of few Australian political leaders with an intellectual grasp of the three-tiered world. It is remarkable, but unfortunately typical of the state of Australian political life and its attendant media, that, in the intense scrutiny of him since he became Leader of the Opposition, unravelling his private life, his attitude to the United States and balanced budgets, almost no attention has been given to his book *Civilising Global Capital* published in 1998. This is a hefty, detailed and sometimes indigestible work in which, however, he accepts the efficiency of globalisation and the inefficiency of the welfare state, in the manner described earlier of Clinton, Blair and Schroeder, and shows a grasp of the forces at work outside his Labor constituency. It is hard to imagine from reading this book that he is not challenged by the complexity of the contemporary world and the opportunity a young country like Australia has in tackling afresh the ancient dilemmas of peace and war. He has had a crash course in defence and foreign policy from which he would have learned that, while as a national leader he should be wary of utopian one-worldism, realism and patriotism can be crackpot as well.

From the positions they have adopted for election purposes, Labor and Democrat governments would look for more international security support on Iraq, but we do not know at this stage what will need to be done. We know that security will remain a concern. We know that the religious communities do not easily work together. We might be facing a civil war in Iraq, or a surrogate civil war, after our elections and before theirs. It is understandable and even, in the longer term interests of the alliance, valuable that outrage at the way the alliance has been abused and mishandled should be maintained, but it remains a fact that the problems created by the invasion will have to be resolved. What we don't know at this stage is whether the problems will be of manageable or catastrophic proportions, and how new governments in Australia and the United States will need, as a test of crisis management, to deal with them.

★

In perhaps an unguarded moment, the Prime Minister once expressed the wry hope that the war against terrorism would not last as long as the Cold War, which lasted for more than forty years. If the metaphor is right, is there a lesson to be learned from the defeat in Vietnam and the awkward and contentious legacy of Iraq? The comparison is suggestive in some respects. Then, as now, the Australian government of the day had no control over the conduct and consequences of the war. It had urged the Americans into Vietnam, following the advice of its threat experts that the safest way of ensuring our defence was to insert US forces on the ground between us and the communist tide. For a while our counter-insurgency experience in Malaysia gave us access in Vietnam to American military planning but any initial influence we had declined as the huge American war machine moved into action. And later, our rhetoric had become so fixed and so dependent on the assumption that any questioning of our role in Vietnam would hurt the alliance with the United States, that we seemed incapable of taking account of what was actually happening. It was obvious that the Americans were in turmoil and, even after the victory of Richard Nixon in 1968, were looking for a way out, as shown by the backdoor diplomacy with Hanoi and the famous Kissinger visit to China. John Gorton made an effort to adjust, but that was one of the reasons he was deposed. Australia was trapped by the insignificance of its presence in Vietnam compared with that of the United States, the fact that the US was a global power with a wide range of responsibilities we did not share and, all the time, the abiding sensitivity that the alliance was of much greater value to us than it was to them. It required a change of government in Australia for a fresh start.

After Vietnam, there was a substantial rethinking of foreign and defence policies in the United States and in Australia. It is time to put on our thinking caps again. Iraq could be a more substantial error than Vietnam, in the sense that it opens up a prospect of fresh conflict, while Vietnam was at the tail-end of a conflict that had begun to settle. The Vietnamese had been fighting a war of independence with the French for years when the Americans intervened, after the military defeat of the French at Dien Bien Phu and the subsequent negotiated agreement at Geneva, splitting the country in two with national elections to follow (on which the US incidentally reneged).

The year 1975 was a turning point in the history of the Cold War. It was the year when American forces finally withdrew, in humiliation, from Vietnam. It was also the year of the Helsinki Accords, which for the first time brought human rights into play as a diplomatic asset for the West. The Europeans got human rights onto the negotiating table with the Soviet Union at Helsinki, forcing Moscow to give some licence to a growing volume of domestic dissent if it wanted the benefits of new economic and security arrangements with the West. The United States, in the *realpolitik* era of Nixon-Kissinger, agreed reluctantly, but elections the following year brought in the Carter administration, which was enthusiastic about human rights. The pressure it applied on the Soviet Union gave dissidents like Andrei Sakharov legitimacy and speeded up the process that brought reformer Mikhail Gorbachev to power between the years 1985 and 1991. Ronald Reagan, who bundled Carter out in 1980 and served for two terms, had to deal with Gorbachev and it is said on his behalf that his military pressure on the Soviet Union, especially the decision to put intermediate missiles into Europe, brought about the collapse of the Soviet Union. It is possible to read the sequence of events differently. Gorbachev and Reagan sought and found common ground on dismantling their intercontinental nuclear weapons systems. It was for this and other co-operative diplomacy that Gorbachev received the Nobel Peace Prize in 1990. And it was "perestroika", and "glasnost", the comprehensive reform of both the economy and political system of the Soviet Union, that aroused so much internal opposition to Gorbachev. A reaction against him by the old guard, a failed coup, the seizure of power by Boris Yeltsin, who had left the communist party and was a popular politician within the Russian Republic, brought an end to the Soviet Union.

In other words, defeat for the US in Vietnam did not mean defeat in the Cold War. Rather, a change of course assisted the United States to win it. There are some similarities here with the war on terror, although the differences need to be kept in mind. Communism had the support of two major powers, Russia and China, each of them nuclear-armed. Terrorism today has no substantial hinterland, only cells and fugitive leaders. All of the world's powerful states are anxious, each for different reasons, to contain it. There are no indications of manoeuvring against Washington. The unpopularity of the United States beyond the circles of Muslim extremism is of its own making.

There is at present a vacuum of leadership at the third tier. The opportunity would seem to be even greater than during the Cold War for the United States – and, one hopes, for Australia – to show leadership on a global scale, countering terrorism not by relying on military power but by exposing its credentials. This is done by addressing where possible the conditions that sustain it, including the conflict between Israelis and Palestinians, and in responding to its desperate brutality not in kind but with the full force of law and order. It is a slow, less dramatic and politically more complex strategy than sending troops to invade some unfriendly country, but it is likely to be more productive. Australia has already begun the process in co-operating with Indonesia for civil and legal action over the Bali bombings and by nipping in the bud what might have become a haven for terrorists in the Solomon Islands. What needs now to be done is to use whatever influence we have with the United States through the alliance to change course in this direction.

⋆

Prompted by an outside event, a review of the alliance is more likely, however, to be from the inside and, because the United States has larger matters on its mind, the initiative will need to come from Australia. It will likely be more fruitful if there are changes of government in both Australia and the United States, but the suggestions that follow are made no matter how the elections are decided.

- The first step is to take the political heat out of the alliance.

It is healthy to debate alliance issues in public. It is unhealthy to turn the alliance into a holy grail. I have said earlier where I think the blame lies, but clearly both, or all, sides of politics need to take the lesson to heart. A depth of distrust, deception and political point-scoring has been exposed and Australian politics and government is the poorer for it.

Public debate will happen anyway, in the media, academic journals and the privately and publicly funded think-thanks that have recently been established. Something more formal might be considered, however, like a joint sitting of parliament, in which the party whips are removed and individuals encouraged to speak freely, or a public forum along the lines Hawke convened to discuss taxation and industrial policy. Much anti-Americanism in Australia feeds on a feeling of impotence and thwarted idealism, which is confirmed by making the alliance unassailable. Whatever the form of debate, the need is for those who value the alliance to make the case for a fresh mandate, not in the language of past battles fought, although their lesson cannot be forgotten, but in the light of the challenges that lie ahead. The case needs to be made not behind closed doors, or cupped hands, but in open discussion.

- Our intelligence relationship with the US needs an overhaul.

Some useful suggestions are made by Philip Flood in his report in July 2004 of the inquiry into Australian intelligence agencies. Many of his recommendations are managerial and professional and some are made only in a confidential version to the prime minister but, in the public report, his appeal for more "contestability" is suggestive. He writes:

> Contestability of advice is a hallmark of the information age. It strengthens policy making and is highly valued in Australian intelligence assessments by ministers, senior officials and operational commanders alike … But contestability mechanisms are not being used to best effect: to give greater authority to decision makers by presenting considered alternative interpretations or judgments, or the most rounded single interpretations.

You can say that again. In the closed-circuit world of intelligence, the occasional shot across the bows is salutary, and Flood suggests ways in which contest, challenge and dissent could be improved. The high priority which secret intelligence has in the official process gives it an influence in government which the quality of its information does not always warrant. It is assumed that *because* intelligence has been secretly obtained it is more accurate than what is known by normal means and more useful in the formulation of policy. Clearly this is not the case. Intelligence varies greatly in quality. Sometimes – as in the Cuban missile crisis – it is decisive in giving political leaders options. Sometimes, as in the absurd "Bay of Pigs" plan in 1961 to invade Cuba that Kennedy inherited, it is romantic. A great deal of intelligence by its nature is self-serving. Information the Americans had about weapons of mass destruction in Iraq seems to have come mainly from an exile who had an interest in getting the Americans to invade his country, remove Saddam Hussein and put him in charge. Why, in this case, was intelligence based on a suspect source preferred to that of a team of professional UN investigators who had been probing every nook and cranny of Iraq for years? Mostly, as in the disintegration of the Soviet Union, the fall of Suharto, the Sandline affair in Papua New Guinea or the various coups in Fiji, it is a small, even indistinguishable, piece in a jigsaw.

In government in several different capacities I never saw intelligence material that was conclusive or analytically superior to any that I had not already acquired from other government material, as from other departments, including Defence and Foreign Affairs and Trade, for example, or from scholarly journals and the media. More racily written perhaps, and the personal gossip was always a good read, but not distinctive as material for the formulation of policy.

Australia has two important relationships where diplomacy is compromised by a high degree of sensitivity over intelligence. Our relations with Indonesia are overshadowed by Indonesia's knowledge that our intelligence technology is a class above theirs, especially our capacity to intercept communications. The suspicious attitude of some influential Indonesians to our promotion of East Timor's self-determination can be partly explained by their conviction that we were setting up a listening post. Our relationship with the United States suffers from our knowledge that the intelligence connection is much more important to us than to them, which inclines us to keep quiet diplomatically while we are in front. The tragic and strange suicide of intelligence officer Mervyn Jenkins in Washington can only be explained by a heightened, even unrealistic, sense of the importance of the intelligence connection.

- Australia's diplomatic resources need to be strengthened.

Defence and especially the intelligence agencies have done well out of the turbulent twenty-first century, while our diplomats have lost ground. The combined budget of the intelligence agencies has doubled from $332 million in 2000–01 to $659 million in 2004–05 and Flood recommends more. Personnel numbers are up from 2301 to 3324. Although it was not his job to report on overt, or diplomatic, reporting, Flood notes that, due to reduced foreign affairs budgets over years, it has declined. He flags a need for more foreign languages. He is currently chairman of the Australia–Indonesia Institute, established to foster non-government, people-to-people social and cultural contact. Although he is too professional to mention it, the institute's budget is less now than when it was founded in 1989. He flags also the desirability of intelligence connections outside the valued US and UK partnership. He does not name them, but they would certainly be in our region.

I am indebted to a former colleague, Geoff Miller, for a thoughtful comment in the *Australian Journal of International Affairs* (which he attributes to Kissinger) that diplomacy is not like engineering, coming on a problem, solving it and moving on. It's more like gardening, cultivating relationships, so that if you need one, it's there.

American diplomacy under Bush has the impact of a front-end loader. Australian diplomacy is of the gardening variety, or perhaps, at times, of the architectural kind. The alliance becomes an impediment if it lulls Australia into a false sense of security and inactivity about our region. It is not a matter of putting up our hand and asking our neighbours to be admitted. It is a matter of working with them to define the region in ways that include us with everyone else. That is the message of successful Australian regional diplomacy in APEC, ARF and the Cambodian peace process.

Australia's interest in global security also needs attention. It seems self-evident that the United States cannot do everything, nor should it be allowed to try. Australia has no influence, or very little, over the global behaviour of the US. However, at the moment it shares some of its unilateralist temper, not because it is powerful like the United States but because the ideas that are part of the currency of debate in Australia do not easily cross the cultural divide to our neighbours.

Australia still stands with the US on some of the fundamentals of sovereignty, bolstered by the additional legitimation that our sovereignty is democratic. The Europeans have taken national sovereignty a step further, trading it for access to a greater regional good, but Australia and the United States both presently stand firm, for different reasons, on state sovereignty.

Australia should return to an earlier interest in multilateral diplomacy, including arms control and disarmament. It should become more active in the UN, including working for the reforms shown necessary by recent events. Australian inactivity at the UN in recent years has been a surprise to those aware of our hyperactivity in the past. The UN is out of favour in alliance circles at the moment, but, as shown in giving legitimacy to the Iraqi interim government, it is still a necessary, if not sufficient, instrument in establishing order and keeping the peace. It is unwieldy, but not unmanageable. It is slow in mounting "blue helmet" operations, but not in approving "coalitions of the willing" when there is political support for them. The crucial mistake over Iraq was not in assembling a coalition outside the UN, but in the clumsy, impatient and even arrogant manner in which UN approval for it was sought.

We should recover the activist and optimistic style of the early post-Cold War period. Australian diplomats have shown themselves to be skilful operators of both global and regional systems. The present terrorist scare is not an eternity: it is a mere blip on the screen of powerful vistas and undercurrents that surfaced at that time. On the other hand, the intelligence agencies, for all their utility to the state in fighting its enemies and contending with its rivals, are not confident players of the three-tier system. Rather, they feed the incipient pathology of the sovereign state and the fears of its people. Indeed, it is in the secret state that deepest opposition to international transparency lies. We now know that the CIA persistently overestimated the threat of the Soviet Union during the Cold War, and in today's circumstances the temptation remains. Governments, unfortunately, have become so addicted to the product of their intelligence agencies that it takes unusually strong and confident political leadership, backed by penetrating and authoritative diplomatic reporting, to keep the covert message in perspective.

- In dealing with terrorism we have a particular set of conditions in our neighbourhood.

Our military forces and our intelligence agencies need to adapt to a world in which terrorism, not a hostile power or combination of powers, is the challenge to national security. As strategic analyst Hugh White has noted, the question arises whether our defence forces should concentrate on war-fighting or peace-keeping and "low-level" security tasks. The answer, inevitably, will be both. As earlier noted, there is no threat scenario at present or indeed has been for some time that contemplates the actual invasion of Australia, but the lead times in defence procurement are so long and the product so expensive that changing course is like rebedding a river. The emphasis now on terrorism, however, directs attention to the lower end of the spectrum, where there are certain regional dangers. The archipelago to our north is a confluence of piracy and smuggling. The oil and gas fields that East Timor inherited need protection, which East Timor alone cannot provide. And there is the threat to Australian lives and property from Islamist terrorism itself.

We are dealing here not with heavily armed enemy states, but with states, and especially Indonesia, which have terrorist organisations in their midst and because of cultural and religious tendencies, not to mention poverty, have difficulty containing them. Pre-emptive military action is no answer. An anti-American sentiment has developed in Indonesia, and also an anti-Australian sentiment, which, though always latent, is now more dangerous because it finds expression not in the declarations of presidents or the actions of military leaders, with whom we have dealt in the past, but with extremists who move among the people. That we have as our close neighbour the most populous Muslim nation, with evidence already of active terrorist organisations, is one of those stubborn facts of our neighbourhood that has been overwhelmed by the controversy and drama of the interventions in Afghanistan and Iraq. The civil and legal co-operation between

Australia and Indonesia over the Bali bombings is a heartening sign that each of us has kept our nerve. It needs to be intensified with Indonesia and extended to other states.

Indonesia, as always, needs particularly close attention from Australian policy makers. In one sense, Indonesia has been a disappointment to those who followed its fortunes from the beginning. It has not developed technologically in the way, say, India has, nor industrially in the way, say, China has. The close association of the military with politics has held Indonesia back from taking advantage of the global opportunities of the post-Cold War era. Indonesians themselves recognise that the hopes of the professional and business middle class that emerged with such intellectual brilliance after independence have been lost in an easy life of soft consumerism, while the nation stagnates.

From Australia's point of view, however, as a neighbour, a comparison of Indonesia with Yugoslavia is reassuring. Indonesia, non-aligned like Yugoslavia during the Cold War, has also suffered since from international fragmentation. East Timor has broken away and Aceh and West Papua are pressing for the same result. Indonesia is as unnatural a nation as Yugoslavia, which was hastily put together after the First World War. Like Yugoslavia it is on a cross-roads, in its case a cross-waterways. In Asia, only India is more culturally diverse, but India has a natural unity created by mountains to the north and sea to the south. Indonesia is an archipelago of thousands of islands straddling a maritime freeway between the Pacific and Indian Oceans. Its outer islands are rich in resources and resent the dominance of over-populated and introspective Java, just as Serbia's dominance was resented in Yugoslavia. Aceh has always been recalcitrant, Sumatra (led by some dissident colonels assisted by the CIA) tried to break away in the 1950s, the Moluccas (the Spice Islands) have a resistant Christian community in the south, as did East Timor and as West Papua has now.

But Indonesia is fortunate. Unlike Yugoslavia, it is surrounded by countries, including Australia, that do not want to dismember it. When Slovenia and Croatia put up their hands, Germany and then most European and Western states, including Australia, were quick to recognise their independence. When the Cold War ended, Yugoslavia was a federation of six republics. Only two are left. Indonesia is safer because it is a member of one of the world's earliest and most successful regional associations, ASEAN, which acts like a cushion against prods and thrusts from outside. Australia is in a good position to work closely with Indonesia and its ASEAN neighbours on terrorism.

If Australia can involve the United States in counter-terrorism in south-east Asia, well and good, although we are capable of managing the necessary co-operation ourselves. We may need to work closely with the United States in north-east Asia, where the security issues are more traditional, involving both Taiwan and Korea.

Despite Menzies' exclusion of Taiwan from the Pacific region covered by ANZUS nearly half a century ago, our contemporary form of inclusive regionalism includes them both and both of them call for patient and skilful diplomacy, as well as the weight and power of the United States.

- It would seem to follow from all this that Australia's multiculturalism, developed on a bipartisan basis since the Whitlam and Fraser governments, needs to be adopted more rigorously as a national strategy.

It cannot be left to the goodwill of ordinary, decent Australians, who under the stress of religious and ethnic conflict begin to wonder about the loyalty of the people next door. It needs to be clearly restated and vigorously led at the highest political level.

As religion has become, at least for the moment, the battle cry of engagement in so much of the world, Australia needs to be mindful that Christianity is a minority religion in our region. Unlike the United States, which dominates a region that is entirely Christian, or Britain, which is part of a Christian (so far) Europe, we are making our way in a region that is not only non-Christian, but also non-monotheistic, Hinduism, Buddhism, Confucianism and Shintoism being predominant. This underlines the political point that Australia is suited by agreed rules of engagement, rather than by power, moral or military, imposed from outside.

If Australia has a future it is not as an outpost of Western Christendom, but as a society in which the secular values of good citizenship outgun the supranational claims of religion, the tribal demands of ethnicity and, for that matter, the stylish appeal of class. There is no conflict here with the United States, which is also multi-faceted. The difference is that the United States is a global power at rest in a Christian hemisphere. We are middling size, finding our way in a region of almost miraculous diversity.

Democracy also is a contentious issue in our region, which is slowly moving, like the rest of the world, to accept the democratic system of government. Those of us who live in democracies and regard democracy as a universal value find it difficult to believe that any other system can be as sensitive to human needs and dignity. Yet there are societies that, either because they are very small, like Bhutan or Tonga, or very large and still developing politically, like Russia and China, or states like Iran or Pakistan that quibble for religious or cultural reasons, do not accept the full thrust of democracy. And there is always the oddity of India, the world's most populous democracy, now especially remarkable with a Sikh prime minister, a Muslim president and an Italian-born Catholic as leader of its most famous political party, but which has never been comfortable with the United States because of its geo-strategic preference for India's enemies. Australia does not need to resile from its belief that democracy is the highest of the political vocations. Even at this early stage of democracy's global evolution, it will find that most of the world's people and most of the world's states agree with it. Yet to force others to change their regimes by using the military muscle of the alliance is a step too far. Yes, Japan is a former enemy who is now a democratic ally, but we do not want to have to go through a war to make the case again. We have to accept that, as the saga of the hanging chads and tampered electoral rolls in Florida for the 2000 US presidential election suggests, democracy is a many-splendoured thing, slow to mature.

Conclusion

It doesn't have to be fatal, but there needs to be a ground shift in Australian politics for the danger to pass.

If we wish, we can declare ourselves to be deputy sheriff in our region. We can proclaim our right to strike pre-emptively. We can help the United States create a national missile defence screen. We can intensify our military and intelligence links with Washington. We can go anywhere in the world as optional military extra. No-one is going to invade us if we do these things, although we might become a more visible terrorist target. And it is just possible that we might make ourselves indispensable to the United States, so that, if we are invaded, they will be on hand to help.

But this is overselling the alliance, pushing an Australian public, already a willing consumer of American goods, services and culture, into an emotional and material engagement with our great and powerful friend that is neither necessary nor prudent. The alliance is in danger of becoming not just a security arrangement between two countries but a test of how as

Australians we see ourselves, the world and the future. Our maturing as a nation had led us to believe that we had developed an autonomy of outlook, an independence of spirit, co-operative but not submissive.

To repeat: Australia benefits from the alliance with the United States which is why, pragmatically, we should keep it. The practicalities of Australia's geopolitics argue for it. The power and influence of the United States in the world are a valuable asset. Australia will not readily give up the advantages it has gained over a long period by its military association with the United States, no matter which political party governs in Canberra. There is an advantage to us at the high-technology end of our intelligence links with the US. There is some, incomplete, assurance in the ANZUS treaty if we are attacked. An American military presence in our region is accepted as contributing to a stable equilibrium. Without it, rivalry between Japan and China and perhaps others might surface. It is not an impediment to our trading and investment prospects, as shown in the recent gas and oil deal with China, nor does it prevent us from working on sensitive political and security issues, as shown in dealing with Indonesia over East Timor. As an economy and as a creative industrial and scientific society the United States is magnetic, and on human rights Australia has more in common with the United States than with most other countries in our region. Also, while the Australian public favours the "idea" of self-reliance, its capacity to bear the costs is not self-evident. We have had defence on the cheap. Without the alliance, there would be a revival of the nuclear weapons option.

In theory, we could disengage from the alliance, as New Zealand has done. In practice, however, we have no need. The choice is not whether or not we have the alliance but how we manage it, whether we use it to exert American power in pursuit of American objectives or whether we use it to promote common interests, including ours and the security of our region. We should try to engage the Americans in arrangements with others that contribute to regional and global security, including a counter to terrorism likely to be more productive and less disruptive than at present. In doing so, we have no need to submit ourselves to some kind of test of loyalty to America itself.

The activism we discovered in ourselves when the Cold War ended included coalition building, but it had other qualities. One was a commitment to thinking and acting internationally. By their nature, middle powers like Australia lack the capacity to get their own way in the world, so they have an interest in a rules-based system which they have some say in establishing. Their manner is co-operative rather than assertive. They are able to see a way through impasses and to lead, if not by authority, then at least by the force of ideas. In other words, if you're not powerful you need to be imaginative, which great powers are reluctant to be. To do so would suggest that they do not value enough their prime possession, which is their power and the authority that comes with it. Middle powers, on the other hand, especially when, as in most cases, they have no hope of becoming great powers, rely on the appeal of ideas in statecraft. Ideas are not enough; the resources and the energy to implement them in a practical way are also needed. An active middle power needs a competent diplomatic service, as well as discretionary funds. It needs, above all, stamina. But, as the old ideas of statecraft fail to work in the contemporary world, imagination is an essential starting point, and imaginative solutions to the pressure of state sovereignty on the land and waters of our region, unlikely to respond to pre-emptive military pressure, is a priority for Australia.

For example, a snapshot of the Asia-Pacific region shows many separatist or nationalist movements which test the status quo: Bougainville, Papua, Aceh, Tibet, inner Mongolia, Xinjiang, the Shan states in Burma, Muslim dissidents in southern Philippines, the Tamil north of Sri Lanka, Kashmir. Japan and Russia contest the Kuriles and almost everyone in south-east Asia makes a claim to the Spratleys. These all present opportunities for solutions not tied to notions of sacred soil and stand-and-deliver heroism. There are examples of dynamic sovereignty, such as China's "one country-two systems" response to the issue of Taiwan's status. A divided Korea needs a settlement somewhere between economically costly reunification and militarily costly separation. Self-government (with external affairs remaining in the hands of another or other powers) was often suggested before the crisis in East Timor that brought independence. Free association (full independence but handing over certain matters, usually external affairs) is in force between the Marshall Islands and United States, the Cook Islands and New Zealand, and has been proposed by the Dalai Lama as a solution for Tibet. Dual sovereignty has been suggested as a solution for the Kuriles Islands. Confederation, where independent states come together in a regional group to which certain additional power is given, and other variations of interdependence have been proposed for some Pacific islands.

Some of these abnormalities could become threats to our security, requiring application of the alliance, but mostly they challenge our diplomacy and, above all, our imagination. The state's attachment to territory has prevented it from adopting the kinds of solutions that business has long used to settle issues of land ownership. When land became too expensive for single ownership, it was sub-divided. When multi-storey buildings were erected to justify the cost of land, strata and company titles were devised. Rental and lease, body corporate and time-share have evolved to meet practical needs. The state, however, is built on hallowed ground. The surface of a good deal of the earth is fertilised with the blood and bones of those who have sacrificed their lives defending the territory of the "motherland" or "fatherland". The combination of territory and sovereignty when associated with powerful emotions makes the state physically inflexible in meeting the competing demands for space. These demands are increasing. The usual response is partition, creating smaller states also territorially bound. The security of these small states (the Democratic Republic of East Timor is of particular interest to Australia) needs to be underwritten or underpinned in ways that have not yet been decided.

Globally, there is an evolutionary shift in the system of states that has given us the ground rules for war and peace for more than three centuries. If the twentieth century has a single lesson, it is that military power has overwhelmed the integrity and authenticity of the state. In defence of its independence, the state has built weapons of mass destruction with global reach. It needs military forces for its own defence, but not weapons that threaten the lives and livelihood of people everywhere, even human existence. If it were once true that states made war and war made states, it is a proposition now ripe for recycling. Even if war can be restricted to the fighting services, "killing each other's children", as described by Jimmy Carter when receiving the Nobel Peace Prize, is not a foundation for peace. The influence of military values in government ceases to be an asset in a world in which economic and social development is primary, international policing is becoming more necessary, and knowledge of evolving global politics and culture is useful in finding a niche for one's country.

A lead has come from the Europeans, who, having knocked themselves out with war, have discovered the benefits of co-operation and are no longer dazzled by the allure of sovereignty. They are learning how to submerge notions of sovereignty and national identity in forms of regional and global co-operation. In our region, Japan is especially interesting. It sought to emulate the modern Western state, with disastrous results. Deprived of the right to make war by a constitution imposed on it by its former enemies, it has bridled occasionally at being merely an "economic animal" in a world of full-bodied martial states, but it has also demonstrated the benefits, becoming the second largest economy. Lately, it has shown an interest in being active in international peace-keeping and it will be encouraging, despite the political controversy at home, if it continues to think of itself in this respect as a vanguard state of the twenty-first century.

The states likely to prosper in the future are not those that seek war as a test of their independence but those that respond successfully both to the human demands from within their boundaries and the opportunities for international co-operation from without. The successful state will repay the loyalty of its citizens with higher living standards and access to a world wider than their defined territory, rather than by going for glory. It will still need the respect of other states, but it will gain this not by brandishing its military might but by forging common interests and accepting a common destiny.

How to get Australia's military alliance with the United States to fit into this future is a task awaiting political leaders on both sides of the Pacific. The current "war" on terrorism has distracted us from other tasks. The United States, still smarting from the September 11 attacks, is not currently in the mood to think outside traditional international security, including military alliances, but there is a role both regionally and globally for Australia in this emerging world, in which power is diffused and the organisation of security requires skilful management and understanding of the three-tier system. So we keep the alliance, but we do not submerge ourselves in it or submit ourselves to tests of our fidelity.

I have written in the belief that we see ourselves as a different kind of nation from the Americans, with something more to give the world than a pale version of the virtues that have made the United States great. Robin Boyd said it well during an earlier time of trouble. We are something more than *Austerica*, a cut-price, austerity version of America, with a dash of hysteria thrown in when we think we are not up to scratch. History and geography have moulded us differently. The US won its independence by revolutionary arms and its people fought each other in a terrible civil war. Its commercial vigour is legendary. Australia got its independence a century later from a distracted and benevolent Britain without a shot being fired. Our public enterprise has been as enterprising until recently as our private enterprise, and there is a residual respect for the state as social safety net and redistributor of wealth. Our kind of modernity is more eclectic, more post-modern than the thrusting core values that drive the United States. And, as earlier noted, our political geography is vastly different. The Americans are dominant in their hemisphere. We have to accommodate to ours.

Yes, we have a history of looking for protection from our neighbourhood. Yes, we have a history of copying the manners of those who protect us. However, we have not become a predatory warrior state and our expeditionary valour has helped to keep alive a sense of responsibility for the world beyond our shores. A powerful, perverse region and an impenetrable, intransigent country have forced us back on ourselves, and we have discovered a resourcefulness. In our region, we have worked our way into a kind of familiarity, still short of integration but no longer apart. Our needs now are no different from our neighbours. We want to keep our individual identity, live in a secure and prosperous neighbourhood and have access to the wider world. The alliance with the United States needs to support those needs, not raise doubts about them.

ENDNOTES

1 William Finnegan, "After Seattle: Anarchists get organized", *The New Yorker*, 17 April 2000, p.41.

2 James D. Wolfensohn, Remarks at the Tenth Ministerial Meeting of UNCTAD: "Rethinking Development – Challenges and Opportunities", 16 February 2000.

3 The New York Times, *The Pentagon Papers*, Bantam Books, New York, p. 63, 1971.

4 George W. Bush, Address to a Joint Session of Congress and the American people, Washington D.C., 20 September 2001, http://www.whitehouse.gov/news/releases/2001/09/20010920-8.html.

5 Samuel P. Huntington, "The Lonely Superpower", *Foreign Affairs*, 78:2, p.43, 1999.

6 Henry Kissinger, *Diplomacy*, Simon & Schuster, New York, p.222, 1994.

7 Sir Eyre Crowe, "England the Holder of the Balance", 1 January 1907, Reprinted in George A. Lanyi and Wilson C. McWilliams, *Crisis and Continuity in World Politics*, Random House, New York, 1966.

8 Hendrik Hertzberg, "Manifesto", *The New Yorker*, 14 October 2002.

9 Mike Allen, "Ex-US military chief blasts Pentagon", *The Age*, 25 May 2004, p.8.

10 George Tenet, Remarks to the United States Senate Select Committee on Intelligence, Washington D.C., 6 February 2002.

11 Minister for Trade, The Hon Mark Vaile MP, Speech on the occasion of the Signing of the Australia-United States Free Trade Agreement, Washington D.C., 18 May 2004.

12 Tim Colebatch and Marian Wilkinson, "Labor warns it may block trade deal", *The Age*, 20 May 2004.

Select Bibliography

BOOKS

Bull, Hedley, *The Anarchical Society*, Macmillan Press, London, 1977

Creveld, Martin Van, *The Rise and Decline of the Nation State*, Cambridge University Press, Cambridge, 1999

Esposito, John L., *Unholy War: Terror in the Name of Islam*, Oxford University Press, New York, 2002

Evans, Gareth and Grant, Bruce, *Australia's Foreign Relations*, (2nd Edn) Melbourne University Press, Carlton, 1995

Everard, Jerry, *Virtual States: The Internet and the Boundaries of the Nation-State*, Routledge, New York, 2000

Friedman, Thomas, *The Lexus and the Olive Tree*, Farrar, Straus & Giroux, New York, 1999

Giddens, Anthony, *Runaway World*, Reith Lecture Series, BBC, 1999

Gilbert, Paul, *Terrorism, Security and Nationality: An Introductory Study in Applied Political Philosophy*, Routledge, London; New York, 1994

Gorer, Geoffrey, *Bali and Angkor: A 1930s Pleasure Trip Looking at Life and Death*, Oxford University Press, London, 1936

Huntington, Samuel P., *The Clash of Civilizations and the*

Remaking of World Order, Simon and Schuster, New York, 1996

Kennedy, Paul, *The Rise and Fall of the Great Powers*, Random House, New York, 1987

Kissinger, Henry, *Diplomacy*, Simon and Schuster, New York; London, 1994

Lindsey, Robert, *The Falcon and the Snow Man: A True Story of Friendship and Espionage*, Simon and Schuster, London, c1979

Morganthau, Hans J., *Politics among Nations: The Struggle for Power and Peace*, Knopf, New York, 1961

Richelson, J. & Ball, D., *Ties That Bind: Intelligence Co-operation between the UKUSA countries – the United Kingdom, the United States of America, Canada, Australia and New Zealand*, George Allen & Unwin, Sydney, 1985

Robertson, Geoffrey, *Crimes Against Humanity: The Struggle for Global Justice*, Allen Lane, London, 1999

Wilkie, Andrew, *Axis of Deceit*, Black Inc., Melbourne, 2004

JOURNALS

Anderson, Jon Lee, "The Uprising: Confrontation with Sunnis and Shia", *The New Yorker*, 3 May 2004

Annan, Kofi, "Two Concepts of Sovereignty", *The Economist*, 18 September 1999

Ash, Timothy Garton, "Europe's Endangered Liberal Order", *Foreign Affairs*, 77:2, 1998

Bayne, Nicholas, "Why did Seattle Fail? Globalization and the Politics of World Trade", *Government and Opposition*, 35:2, 2000

Berger, Mark T., "A New East–West Synthesis? APEC and

Competing Narratives of Regional Integration in the Post-Cold War Asia-Pacific", *Alternatives,* 23, 1998

Betts, Richard K, "Fixing Intelligence", *Foreign Affairs,* 81:1, 2002

Birmingham, John, "Appeasing Jakarta: Australia's Complicity in the East Timor Tragedy", *Quarterly Essay,* No.2, 2001

Brady, Helen, "The International Criminal Court – What's the Future for War Criminals?", *The Sydney Papers,* 12:4, 2000

Burgess Andrea, "The Judgement of Vichy France: An Interview with Sir Ninian Stephen", *Quadrant,* May 1999

Chalk, Peter, "The Evolving Dynamic of Terrorism in the 1990s", *Australian Journal of Foreign Affairs,* 53:2, July 1999

Cirincione, Joseph, "The Asian Chain Reaction", *Foreign Policy,* 118, 2000

Cotton, James "The Near North, the East Asian hemisphere, the Asia-Pacific: Seeking Direction in Australian Foreign Policy", *Australian Journal of International Affairs,* 58:1, 2004

Cox, Michael, "American Power before and after 11 September: Dizzy with Success?", *International Affairs,* 78:2, 2002

Dagi, Ihsan, "Human Rights, Foreign Policy and the Question of Intervention", *Perceptions,* June–August, 2001

Deutch J & Smith, J.H., "Smarter Intelligence", *Foreign Policy,* January–February 2002

Diamond, Larry, "Elections without Democracy: Thinking about Hybrid Regimes", *Journal of Democracy,* 13:2, 2002

Doyle, Michael, "Liberalism and World Politics", *American Political Science Review,* 80:4, 1986

Dyer, Gwynne, "State of War", 23 May 2004, http://www.gwynnedyer.net/articles/Gwynne%20Dyer%20article_%20%20State%20of%20War.txt

Falk, Richard & Strauss, Andrew, "Toward Global Parliament", *Foreign Affairs*, 80:1, 2001

Fuller, Graham E., "The Future of Political Islam", *Foreign Affairs*, 81:2, 2002

Gallarotti, Guilio M., and Preis, Arik Y., "Toward Universal Human Rights and the Rule of Law: The Permanent International Criminal Court", *Australian Journal of International Affairs*, 53:1, 1999

Gannon, Kathy, "Letter from Afghanistan", *The New Yorker*, 22 March 2004

Ganor, Boaz, "Defining Terrorism: Is One Man's Terrorist Another Man's Freedom Fighter?", 23 September 1998, http://www.ict.org.il/articles/define.htm

Gill, Bates & Reilly, James, "Sovereignty, Intervention and Peacekeeping: The View from Beijing", *Survival*, 42:3, 2000

Grant, Bruce, "The Great Pretender at the Bar of Justice", in *The Best Australian Essays 2002*, Black Inc., Melbourne, 2002

Hawthorn, Geoffrey, "Pinochet: The Politics", *International Affairs*, 75:2, 1999

Heisbourg, Francois, "American Hegemony? Perceptions of the US Abroad", *Survival*, Winter, 1999–2000

Helman, Gerald and Ratner, Steven, "Saving Failed States", *Foreign Policy*, No.89, Winter, 1992–93

Hersh, Seymour M., "Chain of Command: Why Did Abu Ghraib Happen?", *The New Yorker*, 17 May 2004

Homer-Dixon, Thomas, "The Rise of Complex Terrorism", *Foreign Policy*, 128, 2002

Huntington, Samuel P., "The Lonely Superpower", *Foreign Affairs*, 78:2, 1999

Ignatieff, Michael, "Is the Human Rights Era Ending?", *The New York Times*, 5 February 2002

Jakobsen, Peter Viggo, "Overload, not Marginalization, Threatens UN Peacekeeping", *Security Dialogue*, 31:2, 2000

Joffe, Josef, "Rethinking the Nation-State", *Foreign Affairs*, 78:6, 1999

Joffe, Josef, "How America Does It", *Foreign Affairs*, 76:5, 1997

Karatnycky, Adrian, "Muslim Countries and the Democracy Gap", *Journal of Democracy*, 13:1, 2002

Kennan, George F., "Morality and Foreign Policy", *Foreign Affairs*, 64:2, 1985

Kennedy, Paul, "The Colossus with an Achilles Heel", *New Perspectives Quarterly*, 18:4, 2001

Kobrin, Stephen J., "The MAI and the Clash of Civilizations", *Foreign Policy*, Fall, 1998

Krasner, Stephen D., "Compromising Westphalia", *International Security*, 20:3, 1995/6

Layne, Christopher, "Kant or Cant? The Myth of Democratic Peace", *International Security*, 19:2, 1994

Lewis, Bernard, "Islam and Liberal Democracy", *The Atlantic Monthly*, February 1993

Mahbubani, Kishore, "The Pacific Way", *Foreign Affairs*, 74:1, 1995

Manning, Chris, "Does Globalisation Undermine Labour Standards? Lessons From East Asia", *Australian Journal of International Affairs*, 52:2, 1998

Manning, Robert A., and Stern, Paula, "The Myth of the Pacific Community", *Foreign Affairs*, 73:6, 1994

Marshall, Joshua Micah, "American Empire Building", *The New Yorker*, 2 February 2004

Martinkus, John, "Paradise Betrayed: West Papua's Struggle for Independence", *Quarterly Essay*, No.7, 2003

Mazrui, Ali, "Islam and the End of History", *The Iranian Journal of International Affairs,* 7:1, 1995

Matthews, Jessica T., "US–EU Estranged Partners", *Foreign Policy*, 127, 2001

Miller, Geoff, "Current and Emerging Challenges to the Practice of Australian Diplomacy", *Australian Journal of International Affairs,* 56:2, 2002

Newland, Kathleen, "Workers of the World, Now What?", *Foreign Policy,* Spring 1999

Pfaff, William, "The Question of Hegemony", *Foreign Affairs,* 80:1, 2001

Pryce-Jones, David, "Savage Gods: Religion, Nationalism and Terror", *The Boston, Melbourne, Oxford Conversazioni on Culture and Society,* 2003.

Quinlan, Michael, "Justifying War", *Australian Journal of International Affairs*, 58:1, 2004

Reus-Smit, Christian, "The Misleading Mystique of America's Material Power", *Australian Journal of International Affairs,* 57:3, 2003

Roth, Kenneth, "Sidelined on Human Rights", *Foreign Affairs,* 77:2, 1998

Sanderson, John, "Major Challenges of United Nations Peacekeeping", *UN University Course on Armed Conflict and Peacekeeping,* Spring 2000

Sen, Amartya and Wolfensohn, James, D., "Let's Respect Both Sides of the Development Coin", *International Herald Tribune,* 5 May 1999

Sen, Amartya, "Democracy as a Universal Value", *Journal of Democracy,* 10:1, 1999

Singh, Bilveer, "The Challenge of Militant Islam and Terrorism in Indonesia", *Australian Journal of International Affairs,* 58:1, 2004

Sinnar, Shirin, "Reflections on the 50th Anniversary of the Universal Declaration of Human Rights", *JUST*, 19, 1998

Slaughter, Anne-Marie, "The Real New World Order", *Foreign Affairs*, 76:5, 1997

Sprinzak, Ehud, "The Great Superterrorism Scare", *Foreign Policy*, Fall, 1998

Strange, Susan, "The Westfailure System", *Review of International Studies*, 25, 1999

Taylor, Paul, "The United Nations in the 1990s: Proactive Cosmopolitanism and the Issue of Sovereignty", *Political Studies*, 47:3, 1999

Verrier, June, "Australia's Self-Image as a Regional and International Security Actor: Some Implications of the Iraq War", *Australian Journal of International Affairs*, 57:3, 2003

Walt, Stephen M., "The Ties That Fray", *The National Interest*, No.54, Winter 1998/99

Waltz, Kenneth, "Globalization and American Power", *The National Interest*, 59, 2000

Weller, Marc, "On the Hazards of Foreign Travel for Dictators and Other International Criminals", *International Affairs*, 75:3, 1999

Wheeler, Nicolas J, "Humanitarian Intervention after Kosovo: Emergent Norm, Moral Duty or the Coming Anarchy?", *International Affairs*, 77:1, 2001

White, Hugh, "Australian Defence Policy and the Possibility of War", *Australian Journal of International Affairs*, 56:2, 2002

Yang, Jiemian, "The Quadrilateral Relationship between China, the United States, Russia and Japan at the Turn of the Century – A View from Beijing", *Pacifica Review*, 13:1, 2001

Index